S. Hrg. 114–308

ISLANDED ENERGY SYSTEMS: ENERGY AND INFRASTRUCTURE CHALLENGES AND OPPORTUNITIES IN ALASKA, HAWAII, AND THE U.S. TERRITORIES

HEARING

BEFORE THE

COMMITTEE ON
ENERGY AND NATURAL RESOURCES
UNITED STATES SENATE

ONE HUNDRED FOURTEENTH CONGRESS

FIRST SESSION

ON

ISLANDED ENERGY SYSTEMS: ENERGY AND INFRASTRUCTURE CHALLENGES AND OPPORTUNITIES IN ALASKA, HAWAII, AND THE U.S. TERRITORIES

TUESDAY, JULY 14, 2015

Printed for the use of the
Committee on Energy and Natural Resources

U.S. GOVERNMENT PUBLISHING OFFICE

95–298   WASHINGTON : 2016

CONTENTS

OPENING STATEMENTS

WITNESSES

ALPHABETICAL LISTING AND APPENDIX MATERIAL SUBMITTED

ISLANDED ENERGY SYSTEMS: ENERGY AND INFRASTRUCTURE CHALLENGES AND OPPORTUNITIES IN ALASKA, HAWAII, AND THE U.S. TERRITORIES

TUESDAY, JULY 14, 2015

U.S. SENATE
COMMITTEE ON ENERGY AND NATURAL RESOURCES
Washington, DC.

The Committee met, pursuant to notice, at 10:06 a.m. in Room SD–366, Dirksen Senate Office Building, Hon. Lisa Murkowski, Chairman of the Committee, presiding.

OPENING STATEMENT OF HON. LISA MURKOWSKI, U.S. SENATOR FROM ALASKA

The CHAIRMAN. Welcome, and good morning. We are at order today in the committee. We are looking at the unique energy challenges that face those who live in the remote and isolated areas that are not connected to our national grid. Alaska, Hawaii, and our territories—these areas are largely dependent on imported diesel fuel for their energy needs. The cost of importing that fuel adds significantly to the overall cost of electricity, and in the case of Alaska, it also adds to the cost of space heat.

Most remote locations pay at least twice the national average for electricity. In parts of my state we see rates that can reach 10 times the national average as a result of the need to import fuel, so when we talk about energy challenges, for us this is every bit as important as anything else that we face. Alaska, of course, is not alone in this. In our isolated areas, in our islands that are reliant on imported energy, this is probably the most debilitating aspect of their ability to have an economy at all.

While the nation's regional grids have a diverse set of energy sources to draw from, most isolated areas simply do not have that luxury. Instead their energy costs are directly tied to the price of oil. Lower prices are providing some relief right now, but energy source diversity is the best and most stable option over the long term. In many parts of our state, the fuel barge comes in once a year, twice a year maybe. Sometimes it does not come when you expect it because you cannot get the barges up the river, but effectively what happens is the communities are locked into the price of fuel at the time that it was contracted. So if you contract for the fuel in July and the prices are reasonable, you enjoy those reasonable prices until the next shipment comes, which may be a year later.

(1)

I asked this morning to see what the people in Bethel paid for their energy costs. In the summer of '13, heating fuel was going for $6.09, diesel was going for $6.51 and gas was at $6.85. In October of '14 we were looking at heating oil at $6.20, diesel at $6.82 and gas at $6.79. We see the low prices around the country. Everyone was benefiting from the low prices, but not so much for those of us in Alaska. We are still seeing price comparisons that simply do not add up.

It is important that we look at remote and isolated energy systems in a holistic manner, not just from a cents per kilowatt hour perspective. In all but a few of the communities served by remote energy systems, economies of scale are simply not a reality. Further, the isolated nature of these energy systems means that they must bear the entire burden of ensuring reliability within the community. The ability to support these energy systems directly depends on the underlying economy, and at the same time, the cost of energy drives that economy.

I was in Pelican over the 4th of July break. Pelican, Alaska is down in the southeastern part of the state, a very small community, with 100 or so people. It is only accessible by boat or by float plane. It was founded as a commercial fish processing site back in the mid-1930's. It processed one million pounds of fish back in 1942, but over the years they have languished as the fish went elsewhere, and they went elsewhere for some pretty simple reasons: ice. If you do not have ice to keep your fish chilled after you have harvested them, you do not have a product.

Making ice takes energy, and without competitive energy, the community could not provide the ice necessary to support quality-based fisheries. The good news for Pelican is that they have a small hydro project that has put Pelican back on the map processing small bits of fish that are coming in, and the fish are no longer going by this community. It is in part due to the fact that they have energy to the school, to the water plant, and now to the fish processors there.

Pelican, in my mind, is an example of how we need to think about energy in these systems. We need to focus on solutions to the problems at hand where energy sources match what the community needs and what the community can sustain, and not simply what is desired for them. From a Federal perspective, we must ensure that our programs do not leave these areas on the sidelines.

I note that the DOE's definition of a microgrid requires the microgrid to be able to disconnect and connect to a larger grid. Well, that is just not possible for those of us in the non-contiguous parts of the United States. We have legislation before the committee, S. 1227, to ensure that the development of microgrid technology includes isolated communities, and hopefully that will become part of our larger energy package.

Finally, I would note that this hearing occurs at the time the Pacific Power Association, which is the umbrella organization for the power companies in the Pacific Islands, including those in the U.S. territories and freely associated states, is holding its 24th annual conference in the Marshall Islands. That is a coincidence, not a matter of coordination, but it is good to know that the issue of remote and isolated energy systems will be highlighted across the globe this week.

The issues associated with islanded energy systems deserve our attention. Energy can be a staggering cost and a staggering burden for the people who live in these areas, so I am pleased that we have set aside time this morning to explore what can be done at the Federal level to help find lower cost solutions to them.

Senator Cantwell, I am going to now turn to you for your comments, but I also want to recognize our colleague, Senator Hirono, a fellow offshore senator. We have had an opportunity in the past to discuss the challenges that are unique to your smaller state and my larger state. While we are at least connected to the mainland, we are clearly islanded in the sense that we are disconnected from the rest of America. I do appreciate working together with you, so if you would also like to make a comment after Senator Cantwell, we would be certainly happy to hear from you as well.

With that, let us go to Senator Cantwell.

STATEMENT OF HON. MARIA CANTWELL, U.S. SENATOR FROM WASHINGTON

Senator CANTWELL. Thank you, Chairwoman Murkowski, for holding this important oversight hearing, and I welcome the witnesses, including our former colleague, Congressman Underwood. Thank you so much for being here. And the Assistant Secretary, thank you for being here. I look forward to hearing everyone's testimony about the challenges of reliable and affordable energy in remote communities in rural Alaska, islands such as Hawaii, and a number of our U.S. territories.

To me this is very important because energy is the lifeblood of any economy. Alaska and Hawaii have challenges as it relates to reliable energy sources, and coming from a state where we have seen cheap hydro build an economy over and over again, I just think this is such an incredibly important issue to how your economies grow in the future.

This committee has jurisdiction over relations between U.S. and the communities of our fellow citizens and nationals who live in the territories. Part of our responsibility is ensuring that these communities have viable economies and that means a need for reliable and affordable energy. We need to look no further than Puerto Rico where electricity costs are over twice the national average, and the public utility is carrying a debt of about $9 billion, to see the consequences of high dependence on costly energy and old equipment.

In other territories or in isolated communities in Alaska, electricity costs are typically three to five times the average of the lower 48 states, and this constitutes a significant challenge to economic development. Two summers ago, Chairman Murkowski and I traveled to remote areas of Alaska, and I saw firsthand the challenges that they face in getting an energy supply and building an economy with these energy challenges, particularly in the winter months. It is a very, very challenging situation.

These communities export cash to operate and maintain their oil-based electric and transportation equipment. Newer, lower-cost electricity generation and transportation technologies are increasingly available, but there are typically two barriers to deployment:

a lack of technical expertise to operate and maintain these new technologies, and these are typically lower income communities which often lack the capital resources needed to finance the transition to less expensive fuel and equipment.

So, partnering with the Federal Government offers ways to overcome these challenges. First, making sure that we tap into technical expertise at the Department of Energy and its laboratories. And second, assuring that these communities can leverage the grant programs administered by the Interior Department's Office of Insular Areas, such as the Empowering Insular Communities Program and Maintenance Assistance Programs. Similarly, the Office helped establish the Pacific Power Association to help island utility officials to learn more and to share their best practices in meeting the challenges of reliable and affordable electricity in these remote communities.

I am glad to have this important hearing today, and thank you again for having this and affording our colleague, Senator Hirono, a few minutes for her comments.

STATEMENT OF HON. MAZIE HIRONO, U.S. SENATOR FROM HAWAII

Senator HIRONO. Thank you, Senator Cantwell. Thank you, Chair Murkowski. I am glad that, Senator Cantwell, you mentioned the high energy costs in Puerto Rico are twice what the national average is. In Hawaii it is three times higher as Alaska is well aware. Senator Murkowski, our two states could become test beds for how we can provide affordable and, in our case, renewable energy to remote areas, something that you and I are very familiar with.

Aloha to my friend, Bob Underwood, President of the University of Guam and former delegate to the U.S. House of Representatives. And, of course, I am really pleased to welcome Mark Glick, the Administrator of the Hawaii State Energy Office, as one of our witnesses today. I am also pleased to see our Assistant Secretary, Esther Kia'aina, another friend who served as first deputy for Hawaii's Department of Land and Natural Resources among positions of public service to the State of Hawaii.

It is incredibly important that we are holding this hearing on islanded energy systems. The people of Hawaii understand the unique challenges that come with living on our islands, but our energy challenges loom especially large. Families and businesses in Hawaii are well aware that they face the most expensive energy costs in the country.

With oil accounting for 80 percent of the energy needs of our state, the people of Hawaii are acutely aware that there be must new alternatives to the volatile prices and vulnerable supply of the global oil trade. We can address our energy needs in ways that are much cleaner using Hawaii's own renewable resources.

In 2008, with the advice and support of the Department of Energy, our state established the Hawaii Clean Energy Initiative, a groundbreaking State/Federal partnership. We set a goal for 40 percent of our energy to come from renewables by 2030, and in June of this year the Governor of Hawaii signed into law an expansion of that goal to—listen to this—100 percent renewable electricity by 2045. This is the most ambitious plan and goal in the country. Can we get there? Mr. Glick is here to tell us how we are going to do that. [Laughter.]

Hawaii has already more than doubled its use of renewable electricity in 6 years to 21 percent. Hawaii also set a goal requiring a 30 percent improvement in energy efficiency by 2030. According to the Hawaii State Energy Office, the standard has resulted in the equivalent of $405 million in energy savings for Hawaii's homes, farms, and businesses. Hawaii has also established an on-bill financing program to help consumers cut their energy costs by investing in clean energy.

Hawaii has benefited from the partnership of the state, the utilities, and the military in finding solutions for an affordable lower carbon energy future. It will help keep at home more than the $5 billion per year that we currently spend on importing energy. So not paying for importing oil and becoming more energy self-sufficient will, of course, mean more money; that $5 billion is circulating in our own economy, creating jobs, raising wages, and helping families make ends meet.

It is great that we are focusing today on how Hawaii and other islanded areas deal with a high dependence on oil, high energy prices, and the reduced reliability of energy supply that comes from not being able to connect our electrical grids and pipelines with neighboring states. At the same time, Hawaii is on the forefront of addressing questions that will need answers all across the state and territories of the U.S.: how to use energy more efficiently in our homes, vehicles, and businesses; how to get affordable energy from increasingly renewable sources; and how to integrate new resources of energy in the energy infrastructure that supports our daily lives.

Thank you, and I look forward to the testimony of our witnesses. Thank you, Madam Chair.

The CHAIRMAN. Thank you, Senator Hirono.

We will now turn to our panel this morning, and welcome to each of you. I will do quick introductions and then we will hear testimony. I would ask that you try to keep your comments limited to 5 minutes. Your full statement will be included as part of the record, and then we will have an opportunity for questions after that.

We will begin the panel this morning with the Honorable Esther Kia'aina, who is the Assistant Secretary for Insular Affairs. As head of the Office of Insular Affairs, Ms. Kia'aina oversees the United States Government's relationship with American Samoa, the Northern Mariana Islands, Guam, and the U.S. Virgin Islands, as well as financial assistance to Palau, the Marshall Islands, and the Federated States of Micronesia through our Compacts of Free Association. Welcome.

We next have the Honorable Robert Underwood. Mr. Underwood currently serves as the President of the University of Guam, but, as has been noted, is a former colleague here. He was the Delegate from Guam to the U.S. House of Representatives.

We are also joined by Mr. Mark Glick, who is the Administrator for Hawaii's State Energy Office, tasked with growing Hawaii's clean energy sector. Mr. Glick has been there since 2011.

We also have Mr. Hugo Hodge. Mr. Hodge is the Executive Director for the Virgin Islands Water and Power Authority, the public power utility for the U.S. Virgin Islands. He is also on the Board of Directors of the American Public Power Association; the Co-Director of the Energy Development in Island Nations, a U.S. Virgin Islands (USVI) Initiative; and, the Chairman of the Caribbean Electric Utility Service Corporation. Welcome to you.

Finally, we have Ms. Meera Kohler. Meera and I were on the plane yesterday coming from Alaska, so I know that she also is clearheaded and not foggy this morning from jet lag. Ms. Kohler has come before this committee several times. She has been the President and CEO of the Alaska Village Electric Cooperative (AVEC) since 2000 and has 36 years in the electric utility business. AVEC serves a population of about 30,000 people across 56 communities with 49 power plants. She is a great friend and one who clearly understands the challenges that we face in Alaska. So thank you for making the long haul.

To each of you this morning, welcome, and let us begin with the Honorable Esther Kia'aina. Welcome.

STATEMENT OF HON. ESTHER KIA'AINA, ASSISTANT SECRETARY FOR INSULAR AREAS, U.S. DEPARTMENT OF THE INTERIOR

Ms. KIA'AINA. Thank you so much. Chairwoman Murkowski and members of the Committee, I thank you for the opportunity to testify on the energy efforts of the Department of the Interior's Office of Insular Affairs (OIA) in the U.S. territories.

The U.S. territories face higher energy costs than the rest of the nation, about three times higher than the U.S. national average. The territories are also nearly 100 percent dependent on imported fossil fuels for electricity generation. To combat these high cost of electricity, the Office of Insular Affairs entered into an interagency agreement with the U.S. Department of Energy's National Renewable Energy Laboratory, or NREL, in 2010 to help the territories of American Samoa, Guam, and the Northern Mariana Islands: (1) establish baseline energy system data; (2) form energy task forces; (3) develop long-term strategic energy plans; and (4) formulate energy action plans. I am pleased to say that all of these objectives have been completed, and we are in the implementation stages of the energy action plans which are living documents that are updated regularly as circumstances change.

On a slightly different track, the U.S. Virgin Islands was selected as the pilot project for the Energy Development in Island Nations, or EDIN, an initiative of the Department of Energy. Interior and the Department of Energy provided technical assistance to the USVI throughout the initiative, and in September 2011, NREL published the U.S. Virgin Islands Energy Road Map which outlines a path for achieving the territory's goal of reducing its dependence on fossil fuel by 60 percent by 2025. As of December 2013, the territory has already achieved a 20 percent reduction in fossil fuel energy consumption, a third of its goal.

OIA's current priority is assisting the territorial governments with the implementation of their energy plans through our Empowering Insular Communities Grant Program at about $3 million annually. Some project highlights include funding support for geothermal exploration drilling programs in American Samoa and the Northern Marianas, a wind pilot project in Guam, solar panel systems for the hospitals on Guam and Northern Marianas, and the integration of a hybrid renewable energy system in American Samoa to bring the Manu'a Islands close to 100 percent renewable by 2016.

The greatest challenge we face is the lack of funding for high priority projects identified in the energy plans. Some of the projects must be supplemented with funding from our OIA's Capital Improvement Project, Technical Assistance Program, as well as our Maintenance Assistance Program, all which are already stretched thin. Another challenge is funding for Puerto Rico. Public Law 113–235 included a provision for energy planning in Puerto Rico that would be funded by the Office of Insular Affairs. NREL's cost estimate for including Puerto Rico is $331,000 for planning purposes. With no appropriation for this effort, OIA's Energy Grant Program would likely suffer for the other territories.

Although the challenges are many, we feel there are still significant opportunities for the territories to reduce the cost of electricity, diversify their supply of energy, and become less dependent on imported diesel fuel. The President's 2016 budget includes $4.4 million for pursuing sustainable energy strategies already identified in the territories' strategic energy plans. Solutions to energy issues are always pressing with significance for the environment, financing of territorial governments, and the well-being of island societies as a whole.

Thank you so much for the opportunity to testify on our energy initiatives in the U.S. territories. With me to help in the answering of any technical aspects of my testimony is Scott Haase, who is the NREL liaison to the Department of the Interior. Thank you very much.

[The prepared statement of Ms. Kia'aina follows:]

STATEMENT
OF
ESTHER P. KIA'AINA
ASSISTANT SECRETARY FOR INSULAR AREAS
DEPARTMENT OF THE INTERIOR

BEFORE THE
U.S. SENATE COMMITTEE ON ENERGY AND NATURAL
RESOURCES

REGARDING ENERGY AND INFRASTRUCTURE CHALLENGES AND
OPPORTUNITIES IN ALASKA, HAWAII, AND THE U.S.
TERRITORIES

July 14, 2015

Chairman Murkowski and members of the Committee on Energy and Natural Resources, thank you for the opportunity to testify on the energy efforts of the Office of Insular Affairs in the U.S. territories. The Office of Insular Affairs (OIA) is responsible for coordinating Federal policy relating to the territories of Guam, American Samoa, the United States Virgin Islands (USVI), and the Commonwealth of the Northern Mariana Islands (CNMI). OIA also administers the financial assistance provided to the freely associated states (FAS) of the Federated States of Micronesia (FSM), the Republic of the Marshall Islands (RMI), and the Republic of Palau under the Compacts of Free Association. Our mission is to help the insular communities by promoting government efficiency, fostering economic development opportunities, and improving quality of life issues.

HISTORY OF THE OIA ENERGY PROGRAM

The U.S. territories face higher energy costs than the rest of the nation. The average residential rate for electricity is about $0.37 per kilowatt hour (kWh). This is about three times higher than the U.S. national average cost of electricity. The territories are also nearly 100% dependent on imported fossil fuels for electricity generation. The cost of imported diesel fuel is not only high, but also volatile, thereby making it difficult for territorial governments to conduct long-term energy planning.

The OIA Process -- with Partners NREL and Territories

To combat the high cost of electricity, the Office of Insular Affairs entered into an inter-agency agreement with the U.S. Department of Energy's National Renewable Energy Laboratory (NREL) in 2010 to help the territories—

  (1) establish baseline energy system data,
  (2) form energy task forces,
  (3) develop long-term strategic energy plans, and
  (4) formulate energy action plans.

Baseline Assessment. In 2011, NREL published initial technical assessment reports that provided baseline energy system data including fossil fuel consumption and costs, electrical generation system profiles, inventories of policies and regulations, and detailed analyses of wind, solar, biomass, waste to energy, and energy efficiency opportunities for each of the territories.

As an example, the following table highlights current energy efficiency and renewable energy opportunities for Guam by designating them a low, medium, or high priority for impact from the Guam Energy Assessment.

Table 1. Energy Efficiency and Renewable Energy Opportunities and Potential Impacts

Opportunity Description	Impact Potential
Create a strategic plan to investigate and implement energy efficiency and renewable energy where technically appropriate and feasible	High
Increase energy efficiency standards in building codes	High
Further development of the Cotal 20 MW wind site with concurrent social acceptance outreach	High
Initiate a cool-roof program	Medium - High
Assess the potential for solar hot water heating in different sectors	Medium - High
Increase energy awareness through island campaigns	Medium - High
Continue to evaluate potential for sea water cooling project	Medium
Establish subcommittee to review options for possible modifications to PL 25-175	Medium
DOD and GPA continue to work together to evaluate the geothermal potential	Medium
Set an energy efficiency standard for island appliances and air conditioning equipment	Medium
Outdoor lighting technology and control improvements	Low

Guam Initial Technical Assessment report, NREL/TP-7A40-50580, April 2011

Territorial Energy Task Forces. Energy task forces in American Samoa, the CNMI, and Guam were established by territorial executive orders in 2011 and met regularly from 2011 through 2013. These task forces were composed of technical and policy experts representing a broad range of stakeholders including utilities, energy offices, academia, commercial sectors, environmental agencies, and legislative bodies. The task forces had the responsibility to identify comprehensive and implementable energy strategies that would reduce the territories' reliance on fossil fuels.

Strategic Plans. In 2013, each of the territories published a strategic energy plan that built on each territory's initial assessment report as well as the meetings of the energy task forces. The strategic energy plans provide island-specific policy options, energy efficiency and renewable energy deployment strategies, education and outreach campaigns, and technology-specific analyses and alternatives.

Action Plans. Shortly after the release of the strategic energy plans, each territory published an energy action plan detailing key strategies that can be implemented in the short term to help achieve goals outlined in the strategic energy plans. The energy action plans include specific actions, timelines, performance metrics, and details of the party responsible for implementing each strategy. The energy plans are meant to be living documents that are updated regularly by the energy task forces as circumstances change.

As an example, the American Samoa action plan lists strategies with their related actions and deadlines:

Table 1. American Samoa Petroleum Reduction Strategies

STRATEGY	ACTIONS	STRATEGY DEADLINE
Strengthen the institutional capacity of ASREC	• Hire a part-time coordinator • Develop proposal(s) for submission to the Empowering Insular Communities (EIC) grant program	July 10, 2013
Make Manu'a 100% renewable energy dependent by 2016	• Deploy photovoltaics (PV) on Ofu and Ta'u • Conduct initial engineering studies for a transition to 100% renewable energy on Manu'a	October 1, 2016
Deploy wind and solar power on Tutuila	• Conduct a prefeasibility study for grid integration • Issue a request for proposal (RFP) for a grid integration study • Determine the viability of issuing RFPs for wind and solar independent power producers (IPPs)	October 1, 2016
Assess the potential for geothermal power on Tutuila	• Conduct preliminary evaluation (Phase I) • Conduct resource confirmation (Phase II)	October 1, 2016
Develop hydroelectric power resources	• Develop a proposal for a feasibility assessment of the Fagatogo Hydroelectric Complex for submission to the EIC grant program • Develop an engineering design/architectural design, and access and trail design proposal, for the next round of funding based on the results of the feasibility study • Develop a restoration proposal for the next round of funding based on the results of the engineering and architectural design work	October 1, 2015

American Samoa Energy Action Plan, NREL Interagency Agreement IAG-10-1773, Task No. WFF41010

Energy Development in Island Nations (EDIN) in the U.S. Virgin Islands

On a slightly different track, the U.S. Virgin Islands was selected as the U.S. pilot project for the international Energy Development in Island Nations (EDIN) initiative due to the territory's high energy prices, its interest in energy efficiency and renewable energy, its close proximity to the mainland U.S., and its manageable size.

The Department of the Interior (DOI) and Department of Energy (DOE) provided technical assistance to the USVI throughout the initiative. In September 2011, NREL published the "U.S. Virgin Islands Energy Road Map" which outlines a path for achieving the territory's goal of reducing its dependence on fossil fuel by 60% by 2025. In accordance with the Energy Road Map, the USVI has implemented several renewable energy and energy efficiency initiatives including solar, wind, landfill-gas-to-energy, liquid propane, biomass energy, and energy efficiency upgrades in homes, schools, and businesses. As of December 2013, the territory has already achieved a 20% reduction in fossil-fuel energy consumption. The EDIN initiative sunsetted in December 2013. However, DOI and DOE continue to support the V.I. through the V.I. Energy Office and Water and Power Authority's V.I. energize Services Unit.

In the summer of 2013, the U.S. Virgin Islands announced the signing of a seven-year deal with Vitol Group to convert their power plants from diesel fuel to liquid propane. The conversion to propane is expected to reduce the USVI's fuel costs by 30% and reduce greenhouse gas emissions by 15%. The Vitol Group will finance all capital costs associated with project construction and the conversion is expected to be complete by September 30, 2015.

Capacity Building Support for the Insular Areas

The Office of Insular Affairs also provides financial support for energy capacity building in the insular areas through its financial support of Pacific Power Authority (PPA) programs and the Pacific Lineman Training Program (PLT). The PPA is an inter-governmental agency that promotes technical training, the exchange of information, and the sharing of management and engineering expertise. Its objective is to improve the quality of power in the Pacific region. OIA funding has been used for engineer capacity building workshops, board member workshops, billing system training, and studies in the insular areas.

As an example, OIA funded a PPA workshop for the Engineers in Demand Side Management (DSM). In the past, there has been limited work by the utilities in energy conservation on the demand side, and this is a critical area for utility focus in their ongoing efforts to reduce fossil fuel consumption. Fossil fuel consumption reduction will help to reduce the amount of imported fuel, which improves economies and sustainability of insular areas.

OIA has also funded the Pacific Lineman Training, which yields substantial cost savings. Improved competency has been documented to improve the system reliability. Equipment failures and power outages are reduced, resulting in lower maintenance and repair costs, and less revenue loss. The system improvements and cost savings are vitally important to the financially struggling island power utilities.

The 2015 Pacific Lineman Training grant will fund 30 weeks of training for a minimum of 82 insular area linemen from American Samoa, Guam, CNMI, Yap, and Chuuk. The advanced training in construction of power distribution systems will enable Chuuk Public Utility Corporation to rebuild properly the distribution system on Weno, in Chuuk State that was damaged during Typhoon Maysak.

IMPLEMENTATION

Empowering Insular Communities

Now that the energy plans have been finalized by the governments of each of the territories, the Office of Insular Affairs' current focus is assisting the territorial governments with the implementation of those plans. The Office of Insular Affairs (OIA) administers the Empowering Insular Communities (EIC) grant program at about $3 million annually. The EIC program was first funded in fiscal year 2011 and has played a crucial role in supporting the highest-priority projects identified in the territories' strategic energy plans. Some project highlights include funding support for geothermal exploration drilling programs in American Samoa and the CNMI, a wind pilot project in Guam, solar panel systems for the hospitals on Guam and the

CNMI, and the integration of a hybrid renewable energy system in American Samoa to bring the Manu'a islands close to 100% renewable energy.

Manu'a. The Manu'a islands are a group of three islands located about 70 miles east of the main island of Tutuila. With the use of EIC funding the American Samoa Power Authority is planning to install a 341 kilowatt (kW) solar panel system along with a battery backup system integrated with the existing diesel generators. Soon after solar panels are installed the utility company will install wind turbines to reach 100% electricity generation from renewable energy. Once complete, the hybrid renewable energy system will be one of the first of its kind in the world.

Commonwealth Utility Corporation. OIA is funding an Integrated Resource Planning (IRP) effort for the Commonwealth Utility Corporation (CUC) in the CNMI for $500,000. The Integrated Resource Plan provides an opportunity for the Commonwealth Utility Corporation to address its current and future energy needs in a structured, comprehensive, and transparent manner. It also provides a chance for interested parties both inside and outside the region to review and provide input for planning decisions. In an effort to arrive at a holistic plan that will meet CUC's long-term energy needs, the IRP will include a comprehensive set of strategies that address plausible resource scenarios and outline the analytical steps needed to objectively evaluate those resource scenarios. Our contractor, NREL, is acting in an advisory capacity, providing both technical and process support.

Guam Memorial Hospital. OIA recently awarded a $500,000 EIC grant award to the Guam Memorial Hospital to install a rooftop solar panel system. As a facility that operates twenty-four hours a day seven days a week, the hospital is one of the largest energy consumers in the territory. The project supports Guam with its energy goal to generate five percent of electricity from renewable energy by December 2015.

DOI Remote Community Renewable Energy Partnership (RCRE)

The Department recognizes that many rural Alaskan communities and other remote jurisdictions in Alaska experience significant energy and infrastructure challenges. For example, of Alaska's approximately 270 communities, roughly 220 are considered rural in that they lack roads and are only served by air or water-borne transportation. Of the 220 rural communities, 180 are primarily or solely reliant on diesel fuel for electricity generation and space heating. This dependence on diesel makes the communities subject to extremely high prices and environmental risk, thus constraining economic growth and self-reliance.

Given DOI's trust responsibility for the many Alaska Native residents of these communities, DOI has recently begun to partner with other federal agencies, the State of Alaska, the University of Alaska's Alaska Center for Energy and Power, local utilities and other interested parties to address the situation. Since 2013, the Department has prioritized the Remote Community Renewable Energy (RCRE) partnership to assist Alaskan rural communities in their energy needs. Led by the Department of Energy's (DOE) National Renewable Energy Lab (NREL) staff, RCRE seeks to replace diesel generation in rural Alaska by developing a standard package of technologies that can more efficiently integrate renewable energy into micro-grids[1].

The initial geographic focus of RCRE in Alaska started with $600,000 commitment. Phase 1a included $300,000 to define the project, conduct market and technical analyses and coordinate with partners at DOD, DOE and State. The next $300,000 will include $200,000 to analyze a village hybrid power and micro-grid system utilizing 20 to 30 percent renewable sources, and how that may be leveraged to a 50 to 75 percent renewable contribution. The remaining $100,000 will be used to develop a detailed analysis of how water treatment and pumping could be used as an energy storage mechanism within the context of these hybrid remote power systems.

The main challenges include developing electronic control systems to maximize the amount of renewable energy that can be placed into the system and right-sizing existing renewable generation and storage technologies. Along with the technology, capacity building for local utilities must ensure that their personnel can monitor, diagnose and address issues with equipment with little local support.

---

[1] A micro-grid serves a small area such as a rural, Alaska Native Village or university campus and may or may not have the potential to connect to a larger grid system such as exists within the so-called "Railbelt", which provides power to 75% of the State of Alaska's population.

RCRE's long-term objective is to develop modular, scalable hybrid power systems to reduce costs associated with the use of diesel fuel in remote, isolated communities. The initial RCRE target is focused on isolated communities below 2 megawatts. The technical objective is to provide up to 75 percent of isolated communities' thermal and electric power needs from local renewable resources, up-to-dated storage and controls, and modern, efficient diesel engines.

For the territories, we in the Office of Insular Affairs are proud of the RCRE Manu'a initiative. The goal is to have one village operating with greater than 50 percent renewables by the end of 2016, and later at 100 percent renewables for all three of the Manu'a islands.

CHALLENGES

Funding. The greatest challenge we face is the lack of funding for high priority projects identified in the strategic energy plans.

Some of the EIC grant projects must be supplemented with funding from OIA's Capital Improvement Project (CIP) and Technical Assistance programs—programs that are already stretched thin. For example, the American Samoa Power Authority is currently installing a 1.2 megawatt (MW) solar power system that is funded entirely with CIP funding amounting to about $1.8 million. In addition, the $2 million Guam wind turbine pilot project is mostly funded with CIP moneys as well as the $1.7 million geothermal exploratory drilling program in the Commonwealth of the Northern Mariana Islands.

OIA's current agreement with the NREL is scheduled to expire on September 30, 2015, and OIA has not yet identified a funding source to continue this important partnership, although some carryover funding may be available.

Puerto Rico. Public Law 113-235 included a provision for energy planning in Puerto Rico that would be funded by the Office of Insular Affairs. NREL's cost estimate for including Puerto Rico is $331,000. With no appropriation for this effort, OIA's EIC grant program would likely suffer.

High and Volatile Energy Costs. The insular areas are currently heavily dependent on imported petroleum for both power generation and transportation. The volatility of fuel prices makes long-term energy planning difficult in all of the insular areas, and affects energy security in the Pacific territories because their primary source of fuel is Asia. Remote locations lead to high shipping charges, which are themselves affected by fuel price volatility as the ships run on petroleum.

High and unpredictable energy project development costs. New energy projects face a number of significant challenges, including:

- The scarcity of local energy sector data for making informed decision.

- Absence of strong local regulations designed to ensure orderly development of energy projects.

- Absence of technical and process expertise for vendor selection.

- High shipping costs and long lead times that slow projects.

- Lack of engagement by the public, landowners, and local leaders that results in a lack of community support.

- Need to engage differing priorities as a single project -- such as energy consumption in the power and transportation sectors, disaster resiliency, solid waste handling, wastewater treatment, and climate change adaptation.

- A lack of enabling policies to reduce fossil fuel consumption and promote the growth of renewable energy – such as effective net metering laws, grid integration strategies, and alternative transportation plans.

- Failure to address post-construction operations and maintenance needs and financing.

OPPORTUNITIES

Although the challenges are many, we feel there are still significant opportunities for the territories to reduce the cost of electricity, diversify their supply of energy and become less dependent on imported diesel fuel. For example, the U.S. Virgin Islands already has achieved a 20% reduction in fossil-fuel energy consumption and has seen a significant drop in energy costs over the past year, with rates dropping from $.51/kWh to about $.39/kWh; V.I. rates may be even lower today.

The President's 2016 budget includes $4.4 million for pursuing sustainable energy strategies already identified in the territories' strategic energy plans. Additional opportunities present themselves:

- Territorial issuance of RFPs to implement ideas already identified in existing energy plans.

- Conducting energy audits, especially of major users, and to implement energy efficiency.

- Collection and analysis of wind and solar data in all insular areas.

- Development or updating of integrated resource plans (IRPs) with the utilities in each insular area to ensure that short-term actions serve long-term needs.

- Development of action plans that simultaneously address the interrelated issues of energy such as climate change, security and disaster resiliency, along with waste disposal and waste-to-energy initiatives.

- Study sustainable transportation alternatives to reduce consumption of petroleum.

- Actions to reduce financing risks for private sector investors and developers.

- Ensure that operations and maintenance needs and financing are addressed along with local workforce training.

- Install prepay meters in all territories to yield savings in electric consumption amounting to 10 to 30 percent.

Solutions to energy issues are always pressing, with significance for the environment, financing of territorial governments and the well-being of island societies as a whole. In recent years, the Office of Insular Affairs has played an important role in ameliorating energy problems in the territories. In the years to come, we expect to continue efforts that lead to new energy solutions.

The CHAIRMAN. Mr. Underwood, welcome.

STATEMENT OF HON. ROBERT UNDERWOOD, PRESIDENT, UNIVERSITY OF GUAM, AND FORMER GUAM DELEGATE, U.S. HOUSE OF REPRESENTATIVES

Congressman UNDERWOOD. Thank you. Hafa adai. Good morning, Senator Murkowski, Madam Chair, and members of the committee. It is an honor to be asked to share some ideas and perspectives on energy issues in remote areas, especially island communities. I am President of the University of Guam since 2008 and former Congressional Delegate, as has been mentioned. Part of the initiative as President is to establish the Center for Island Sustainability to kind of function as an honest broker on issues related to the sustainability of the islands in what we consider our greatest challenge, which is to try to figure out how to sustain our economy, our way of life, and our environmental resources at the same time.

Our greatest export from Guam is money. As soon as we get it, we export it, and $300 million a year, which is roughly seven and a half to 8 percent of our total, what we call our gross island product, goes to fossil fuel. As you have pointed out, Madam Chair as well as Senator Hirono, if we were able to capture portions of that export through efficiencies and through the establishment of renewables, we could keep the money circulating in the Guam economy, generate jobs, improve the quality of our lives, and make significant strides toward energy independence. And that is the holistic approach that we think is necessary for people to understand.

Power generation on Guam is provided by local companies which face significant challenges to keep power constant and consistent due to infrastructure issues, and the fact that we are disconnected from a greater grid, a national grid, a continental grid. They also must try to maintain policies which are able to pay back their long-term indebtedness.

In most instances, the power companies are the drivers of energy policy rather than the entire society, and this is because they exist in a power vacuum. I hate to use that term, but that is exactly what happens in many of the islands. Consequently, strategic planning which engages energy issues as a long-term social and economic issue as well as dealing with technological innovations is incoherent and is really driven by occasional Federal initiatives. Some of the initiatives outlined by the Assistant Secretary have been very helpful, and there are others by the U.S. Department of Energy, and sometimes by the U.S. EPA. But looking at it from an island perspective, what happens is that you see various initiatives coming back and forth, and you are not sure which ones are really indicative of the entire Federal policy toward energy in the insular areas.

Financing innovative technologies is complicated by, of course, capital shortages and the notion, very common, that innovative technologies is a Federal or external responsibility. Island power systems effectively must, of course, function as micro or minigrids. While our solutions to this are simple—well, they are simple to say, not simple to carry out—we need strategic planning which is holistically based and focuses on greater energy independence and the positive consequences which include economic growth and sustainability.

We need to understand the concept of "indigenous energy," bringing back using technology to help build independence. In the experiences of the islands, the introduction of technology usually means greater dependence on the outside world. Energy technology, renewables, actually reverses that trajectory.

We need to adopt strong, but achievable, goals which reward innovation and spur participation rather than skepticism and opposition. This means we need renewable energy portfolio standards which are realistically arrived at but which have rewards and consequences. We need capacity building which is based on people, not just on infrastructure, and education for the work force and community outreach which enhances energy literacy, which goes further than just computing the dollars and cents computation of kWs, as you mentioned in your opening statement, Senator Murkowski.

Federal policy initiative and activities must be coherent and consistent. A multiplicity of funding sources and regulators and technical assistance possibilities do not facilitate coherence in small communities, but rather the creation of silos within those small communities. There is very little followup on the ground by any Federal agency relating to energy in spite of its importance, which means the deploying of individuals from agencies to help us and to help those islands. The Federal Government should provide not only seed funding and technical assistance for some innovative projects but also the establishment of green funds themselves which are sustainable.

Last, we want to call for development of not just an all-island, but an all-islands, solution and network. Individual communities must develop their own coherent policies and initiatives for individual sustainability; however, we must join all-islands networks to share best practices and to avoid redoing what has been done before. We have done this through the establishment of the Center for Island Sustainability and our annual conferences. We have also reached out to remote communities in Alaska through our relationship with the center at the University of Alaska-Fairbanks, which I visited last year.

The committee's efforts and the efforts of our partners, particularly under the leadership of the Office of Insular Affairs and other Federal agencies, will be greatly enhanced by adopting policies which reward demonstrated collaboration, successful projects, and which build that human capacity. A key factor in this is to not just look at territories as political jurisdictions, but to adopt an all-islands approach through the participation of islands, whether they are in the Pacific, the Caribbean, off the coast of Alaska, or the New England coastline.

I will be happy to answer any questions. Thank you very much.

[The prepared statement of Congressman Underwood follows:]

U.S. SENATE ENERGY AND RESOURCES COMMITTEE

HEARING ON ENERGY IN REMOTE AREAS

TESTIMONY

Robert A. Underwood
President, University of Guam
July 14, 2015

Hafa Adai and Good Morning,

It is an honor to be asked to share some ideas and perspectives on energy issues in remote areas, especially island communities. I am Robert Underwood, President of the University of Guam since 2008 and former Guam Congressional Delegate to the U.S. House of Representatives from 1993-2003. During my tenure at the University of Guam, I established the Center for Island Sustainability (CIS) and served as co-chair of the Guam Energy Task Force since its inception in 2009. The GETF was established pursuant to a joint initiative between the Office of Insular Affairs, DOI and the Guam Governor's office,

Our interest in island sustainability is predicated upon the common perception around the world that we are at a liminal moment where the balance between our activities as humans and the sustainability of our natural environment puts both at serious risk. While this is true around the world, it is especially true in small island societies because of the scale of our societies and the reality that almost all strategic thinking about resource, economy and people issues is formulated in large societies and, like so many other facets of human existence, small islands are left to pick and choose what they think may apply. At the University of Guam, we are trying to generate strategic thinking based on an ethical commitment to the sustainability of our island way of life, our natural environment and our economy in equal and mutually supportive measures. For us, this means the conduct of relevant, island-based research and the building of internal capacity to deal with the challenges we face whether it is energy dependence, climate change or human migration.

Island Conditions/Challenges

*Our biggest export in Guam is money. As soon as we generate the funds, we export it to purchase off-island for most of our island needs. This is especially true for energy where we spend over $300 million annually for petroleum-based fuel for our transportation and power needs. This represents approximately 7.5% of Guam's GDP. If we were able to capture large portions of that "export" through renewables and efficiencies, we could keep the money circulating in the Guam economy, generate jobs, improve the quality of our lives, make significant strides towards energy independence.

*Power generation is provided by local power companies which face significant challenges to keep power constant and consistent due to infrastructure issues. Moreover, local power companies must

keep pace with environmental regulations as well as remain responsible stewards of long-term indebtedness.

*Strategic planning which engages energy issues as a long-term social and economic issue as well as a technological matter is incoherent and tends to be driven by federal initiatives. This is complicated by "silver bullet" thinking and adaptation of models from larger societies.

*Financing innovative technologies is complicated by capital shortages and the notion that this is a federal or external responsibility

*Island power systems effectively must function as micro or mini-grids which limit the ability to provide consistent and efficient power

Island Solutions/Successful Policy

*Strategic Planning which is holistically based and focuses on greater energy independence and the positive consequences which include economic growth and sustainability.

*Understanding of the concept of "indigenous energy" and the adaptation of technology which promotes independence of action rather than more external dependence

*Adoption of "stretch," but achievable goals which reward innovation and spur participation rather than skepticism and opposition

*Capacity building which is based upon training and education for the workforce and community outreach which enhances "Energy Literacy" rather than just computes dollars and cents computation of KW's

* Federal policy coherence- a multiplicity of funding sources and regulators and technical assistance possibilities does not facilitate coherence in small communities, but rather the creation of more silos inside small island communities.

*Federal government should provide seed funding and technical assistance for innovative projects but also the establishment of "green funds" which are sustainable.

*Development of all island and all islands solutions and networks. Individual communities must develop their own coherent policies and initiatives for individual sustainability. However we must join "All Islands" networks to share best practices and to avoid re-doing what has been done before. We have done this through the establishment of the Center for Island Sustainability and our annual conferences. We have also reached out to remote communities in Alaska through our relationships with the University of Alaska-Fairbanks campus.

The Committee's efforts and the efforts of our partners in the Office of Insular Affairs, DOI and other federal agencies will be greatly enhanced by adopting policies which reward demonstrated collaboration, successful projects and build capacity. A key factor in this is to look not just at territories or political jurisdictions, but to adopt an "All Islands" approach through the participation in existing networks of support, information exchange and research amongst all island whether they are in the Pacific, the tropical Caribbean, Alaska or the New England coastline.

I will be happy to answer any questions and discuss the UOG experience specifically with various grants and our support of the Guam Energy Task Force.

The CHAIRMAN. Thank you, Congressman Underwood.
Mr. Glick, welcome.

STATEMENT OF MARK GLICK, STATE ENERGY ADMINIS-TRATOR, DEPARTMENT OF BUSINESS, ECONOMIC DEVELOP-MENT, AND TOURISM, STATE OF HAWAII

Mr. GLICK. Thank you. Good morning, Chair Murkowski and members of the committee. Thank you for inviting me to testify before you today about Hawaii's energy ecosystem and the challenges and opportunities faced in operating islanded energy systems in the Hawaiian archipelago.

First, the state views our annual expenditure of about $5 billion a year on imported oil as a tax on growth in Hawaii that imposes a significant burden on our residents and businesses. Economics and energy security have driven our push for clean energy with substantial progress for energy transformation finally taking root, once a bipartisan collage of policymakers in Hawaii's congressional delegation and our Statehouse decided to take bold action. This was embodied in the 2008 Memorandum of Agreement between the U.S. Department of Energy and Hawaii and the subsequent passage in 2009 of the nation's strong renewable portfolio and energy efficiency portfolio standards, something we call the Hawaii Clean Energy Initiative, as Senator Hirono mentioned in her remarks.

In 2013, the Governor established energy policy directives to offer guidance and clarity for actions necessary to fulfill Hawaii's energy transformation. I would like to emphasize directives calling for a diversified energy portfolio and relying on clean energy solutions in which the market decides winners and losers, and the results have been strong. The renewable portfolio topped 21 percent at the end of last year, well ahead of the 2015 interim target of 15 percent, and the state has reduced electricity demand by more than 15,000 gigawatt hours. To do this, we used the winning strategy of paying off infrastructure costs through energy savings, and Hawaii has led the nation for three consecutive years in the per capita value of energy savings performance contracts.

Hawaii also leads the nation in solar capacity per capita, even though our isolated grid cannot absorb the percentage of intermittent renewables through the interconnection with the regional grid as is done on the mainland. So to address these technical challenges and costs associated with incorporating this increasingly large percentage of renewables, our electric utilities are working with the host partners to test and work on specifications of fast trip, inverter functionality to avoid transient over voltage events, Midwich distribution circuit to determine proactively the amount of distributed energy resources that can be hosted on each circuit, and work with inverter manufacturers to bring to market advanced inverter functionality to manage voltage levels to customers.

Now, to support these solutions, our office, the Hawaii State Energy Office, focuses more these days on utility resource planning, rate design, and price signals to inform energy stakeholders on the optimal configuration to achieve a growing portfolio of renewable resources. One example I would like to cite is our modeling of load balancing and storage resources from higher penetrations of electric vehicles.

If we assume 120,000 electric vehicles are operating when we achieve a 70 percent renewable portfolio, peak energy demand, electric demand, would increase by as much as 20 percent, resulting in a 10 percent increase and our need for energy storage. However, if those 120,000 electric vehicles are supported by smart charging and advanced systems to be connected to the grid, energy storage requirements might actually be decreased by 10 percent.

Now, the fact that we are the most isolated population concentration in the world makes energy resiliency and disaster recovery an even greater concern. Renewable energy and distributed energy offers great energy resilience, and we have also taken concrete steps to ensure that Hawaii's clean energy transformation is realized by all demographics and communities throughout the state. That is why our new securitized rate reduction bond and On Bill Repayment Green Financing Program targeting the undeserved residential customers, renters and non-profits, is so important.

So in conclusion, Hawaii has been able to leverage our isolation and the challenges faced in the arena of clean energy to great advantage. Hawaii has been able to attract international investment from governments and corporations who see Hawaii as a bellwether for renewable energy solutions before rolling out to international markets, and this success has prompted the state to rethink the potential of Hawaii's clean energy transformation.

The offshoot was the passage of the bill that Senator Hirono had mentioned signed by Governor Ige in June of this year calling for Hawaii's electric utilities to accelerate the 2020 interim RPS target or renewables from 25 percent to 30 percent, and, of course, go to 100 percent renewable energy by 2045. Our continued refinements of these targets assist in resource optimization and prevents costly overbuilds, and sets a clear, unambiguous goal of generating 100 percent electricity from its renewable sources. Our approach in setting targets for utilities is a practical approach to furthering the state's energy policies.

So thank you for this opportunity to highlight Hawaii's clean energy leadership and to share some of the lessons we have learned in pursuing our clean energy transformation.

[The prepared statement of Mr. Glick follows:]

DAVID Y. IGE
GOVERNOR

LUIS P. SALAVERIA
DIRECTOR

MARY ALICE EVANS
DEPUTY DIRECTOR

DEPARTMENT OF BUSINESS,
ECONOMIC DEVELOPMENT & TOURISM

No. 1 Capitol District Building, 250 South Hotel Street, 5th Floor, Honolulu, Hawaii 96813
Mailing Address: P.O. Box 2359, Honolulu, Hawaii 96804
Web site: www.hawaii.gov/dbedt

Telephone: (808) 586-2355
Fax: (808) 586-2377

Prepared Testimony of
Mark Glick
State Energy Administrator
Department of Business, Economic Development, and Tourism
State of Hawaii

U.S. Senate Committee on Energy and Natural Resources
Hearing on Islanded Energy Systems, Focusing on Hawaii, Alaska and U.S. Territories

July 14, 2015

Good morning Chair Murkowski and members of the committee. Thank you for inviting me to testify before you today about Hawaii's energy ecosystem and the challenges and opportunities faced in operating islanded energy systems in the Hawaiian archipelago. While there are discreet distinctions between islanded and interconnected systems, many of the solutions Hawaii has explored, and in some cases has pioneered, may be broadly applicable to all energy systems and accordingly inform future policies and expenditures at the federal level.

Hawaii's geographic isolation -- roughly 2,500 miles from the nearest land mass -- has played a central role in the evolution of the state's energy system. Even with the recent rapid growth of renewable energy in our electricity sector, more than eighty percent (80%) of Hawaii's energy still comes from petroleum, making us the most oil-dependent state in the nation. For much of the post-war era, Hawaii's over-reliance on oil for power generation had a relatively modest impact on the state's economy and energy security, as crude prices were generally stable. But as global crude markets became more volatile starting with the Arab oil embargo of the early 1970s, Hawaii's dependence on oil became a significant economic liability. Today, Hawaii spends about $5 billion a year to buy foreign oil to support its energy needs. As a result, Hawaii has the highest energy costs among the fifty states. This represents a tax on growth in Hawaii that imposes a significant burden on our residents and businesses.

Economics and energy security were the initial drivers for clean energy plans nearly 40 years ago, but it took more than 30 years for those plans to become actionable policies for greater energy self-sufficiency. There was considerable inertia from Hawaii's historic reliance and interdependence on petroleum as the predominant fuel in all sectors. This was due to the knowledge that downward pressure on petroleum demand in Hawaii's small energy market would adversely affect the delicate product balance of the two local refiners supplying jet fuel, gasoline, diesel, and low sulfur fuel oil. However, increasing calls for greater food and energy security along with a rising sense of the harmful impact of climate change on Hawaii's island communities created the urgency and momentum for change.

Mark Glick Testimony
U.S. Senate Committee on Energy and Natural Resources
Page 2
July 14, 2015

An important best practice pursued by Hawaii was the establishment of its first renewable portfolio statute in 2001, requiring renewable energy as a certain percentage of utility sales. The first major milestone in this regard was achieved in 2009 when the Hawaii Legislature passed a forty percent (40%) renewable portfolio standard (RPS) to be achieved by 2030 and an energy efficiency portfolio standard (EEPS) equivalent to a thirty percent (30%) reduction in electricity use through efficiency and conservation. An important distinction from previous plans was the bipartisan coalition of policymakers in Hawaii's congressional delegation and statehouse, which was embodied in a 2008 Memorandum of Agreement between the U.S. Department of Energy and Hawaii, and was subsequently reconfirmed in 2014.

The new policy agenda and roadmap for action was bolstered by an unprecedented partnership of energy stakeholders, all of which became known as the Hawaii Clean Energy Initiative. The Initiative received a significant amount of financial and technical support for resource assessments, scenario analyses, and wind and solar integration studies from the Department of Energy, the National Renewable Energy Laboratory, Office of Naval Research, and the Hawaii Natural Energy Institute. Knowledge gained by this body of challenging work during the past six years provided greater understanding on how Hawaii's islanded grid systems could operate safely and reliably in Hawaii with unprecedented levels of intermittent renewable power. Also, long-term funding for clean energy and energy efficiency technical assistance at the state level was established through a 25 cent fee on each barrel of petroleum product sold in the state, excluding aviation fuel.

In 2013, the Governor established five Energy Policy Directives to offer guidance and clarity for future policy, regulatory and financial actions necessary to fulfill Hawaii's energy transformation. Under the policy directives, Hawaii's new energy ecosystem should consist of a diversified energy portfolio, anchored in indigenous renewable resources, and supported by an integrated and interconnected energy infrastructure. In addition, clean energy development should balance economically and technologically sound solutions and Hawaii's unique environment and culture. Hawaii should also leverage its role as an emerging international clean energy test bed to attract innovation and investments in the new clean energy sector. Finally, Hawaii's renewable future should not be pursued at any cost, but in an environment in which energy efficiency and clean energy can prevail on the basis of providing superior value to conventional energy sources and systems.

Perhaps because of Hawaii's isolation and vulnerability, these common themes have been universally embraced, and the Hawaii Clean Energy Initiative has grown stronger during the course of three gubernatorial administrations and four biennial legislative sessions. Most importantly, energy consumers and other stakeholders have enabled a growing clean energy market that has expanded at such a rapid pace that Hawaii has greatly exceeded its interim RPS and EEPS statutory targets. The RPS topped twenty-one percent (21%) at the end of last year, well ahead of the 2015 interim target of 15 percent. On the energy efficiency side, the state has reduced electricity demand by more than 1,500 gigawatt-hours. Energy efficiency and demand response are playing a crucial role in benefiting both consumers and electric utilities in a number of ways, including with respect to integration of additional renewable energy resources and improving the efficiency of the State's electric grids.

Mark Glick Testimony
U.S. Senate Committee on Energy and Natural Resources
Page 3
July 14, 2015

When examining the costs of generation, producing electricity by tapping our world class trade winds, abundant sunshine and other renewable resources compares favorably with producing electricity from oil. While clean energy goals in other jurisdictions may conflict with economic goals to lower the cost of electricity, in Hawaii it is clear that the transformation to a clean energy future is entirely consistent with the economic goals of lowering the cost of electricity. Recent utility-scale renewable energy contracts procured by Hawaii's electric utilities for wind, solar and geothermal are below the avoided cost of oil-fired generation. Power purchase agreements negotiated by Hawaiian Electric Company over the past year for utility scale solar and wind range from 14 cents per kilowatt hour to 15 cents per kilowatt hour. That compares with an average oil-fired price of generation of 20.1 cents per kilowatt hour over the past five years. Also, the tens of thousands of Hawaii residents and businesses who have installed distributed PV systems have been able to slash their electricity bills, with some using the savings to pay off their investments in as little as five to six years.

Hawaii has also led the nation for three consecutive years in the per capita value of energy saving performance contracts. These agreements are between a building owner and a private energy services company specifying that future operational cost savings can be used to pay for the entire cost of a building's energy and water efficiency retrofits. These contracts assist Hawaii in mobilizing investments in high-impact energy efficiency projects to help the State achieve its energy targets.

Hawaii's transition to clean energy has not been without its share of technical challenges and costs associated with incorporating increasingly large percentages of intermittent renewable energy, which was most recently experienced by the rapid growth of distributed solar. Today, I cite three examples of how Hawaii is dealing with these challenges, including the interconnection of intermittent power, integrated resource planning, and the growing integration of the electricity and transportation sectors. A final example also discusses energy assurance and reliability challenges in Hawaii's changing energy ecosystem.

Hawaii is leading the nation in customer adoption of distributed solar. The national average is less than 1 percent. Today, Oahu leads the nation at 12 percent, with Maui a close second at 10 percent, Hawaii island at 9 percent and Kauai at 7.3 percent.

The result of this unprecedented growth in solar is that one-third, or 136 of Hawaiian Electric Company's 416 circuits in Oahu are said to exceed 120 percent of daytime minimum load, with 10 percent exceeding 250 percent. At 250 percent, that means that on any given day, there is 2.5 times the amount of electrical generation capacity on a circuit at certain times of the day than the minimum load requirements. This is a particularly challenging problem given that one of the main jobs of an electric utility is to match load with demand.

When one considers that Hawaii also leads the nation in solar capacity per capita, the rates of renewable penetration are even more impressive because Hawaii's isolated grid cannot absorb the percentage of renewables that can be interconnected in states that are attached to a regional grid. Consequently, often at the firm prodding of the Hawaii Public Utilities Commission and other energy stakeholders, Hawaii's utilities have had to act in real time to propose, deploy and confirm solutions for integrating such high levels of renewables. Among the current strategies deployed by Hawaiian Electric Company are:

Mark Glick Testimony
U.S. Senate Committee on Energy and Natural Resources
Page 4
July 14, 2015

- Testing and working on specifications of "fast trip" inverter functionality to avoid transient over-voltage events;
- Computer modeling each individual distribution circuit to determine proactively the DER "hosting capacity" of each circuit; and
- Working with inverter manufacturers to bring to market advanced inverter functionality to manage voltage levels to customers.

These solutions are having an immediate and profound effect on reducing the interconnection queues that were established by the utilities to manage the pace of distributed solar interconnections in the name of system reliability and safety.

A second example is what Hawaii is doing to optimize its energy systems to achieve the new 100 percent RPS by 2045. By becoming the first state in the nation to adopt a 100% renewable portfolio objective by a certain time, Hawaii has effectively defined the end state objective for all future investments in Hawaii's electricity sector.

This allows the planning of systemic change, not incremental change, towards a new clean energy future that is structurally different than the present model. While interim objectives drive investment, all of the steps must be taken in support of the long-term goal. As an example, there may be numerous generation and grid design configurations that support the development of 20% or 40% renewable energy. However, given the type and quality of known or presumed renewable energy options throughout Hawaii, there are clear paths to support a renewable mix at 70% or 100%.

By modeling an even mix of wind, solar and dispatchable renewables such as biomass, geothermal or ocean thermal energy conversion, storage requirements can be reduced by half or more when compared to higher proportions of intermittent renewables, which will result in significant cost savings to ratepayers. The lesson here is that planned optimization at an early stage may limit overbuilding costly solutions and is critical in the long-run containment of costs to upgrade the electrical system.

For these reasons, the Hawaii State Energy Office is focusing on utility resource planning, rate design and price signals to collaborate and inform Hawaii's electric utilities and the Public Utilities Commission on optimal configurations to achieve a growing portfolio of renewable resources, as well as to achieve equitable rates of compensation for installed systems. The goal is simple: working towards 100 percent renewables in a manner that achieves the greatest value for the lowest total cost to all customers.

The third example is how Hawaii is looking beyond the electricity sector by expanding its focus to transportation which accounts for nearly two-thirds of the state's energy mix. Hawaii has just completed a comprehensive analysis on tactics that can be implemented to materially reduce fossil fuel consumption in Hawaii, and has developed a broader energy-transportation stakeholder alliance to collaborate on an energy road map that takes into consideration the growing interdependencies between the transportation and electric sectors.

Mark Glick Testimony
U.S. Senate Committee on Energy and Natural Resources
Page 5
July 14, 2015

To best take advantage of tactics dealing with electric drive vehicles, the state is beginning to model load balancing and storage resources for the electricity sector from higher penetrations of electric vehicles. For example, presuming attainment of a 70% renewable portfolio, the addition of 120,000 electric vehicles on the road would increase peak electricity demand by as much as 20 percent, resulting in a corresponding 10 percent increase in energy storage requirements.

However, if the 120,000 electric vehicles are supported by smart charging and advanced systems to be connected to the grid, energy storage requirements might actually be decreased by 10 percent, despite increasing the amount of renewable energy on the electric system.

Hawaii is also investigating the possibility of hydrogen vehicles to offer similar potential as a form of energy storage since hydrogen can be produced at times when renewable energy is abundant and stored for fueling vehicles at appropriate times of the day.

The fact that Hawaii is the most isolated population concentration in the world makes energy resiliency and disaster recovery an even greater concern and all the more valuable. Catastrophic events such as Hurricanes Katrina and Sandy have reminded the nation of the critical value of energy resiliency and disaster preparedness.

The development of micro grids that leverage renewable energy and distributed energy resource investments can provide additional value by providing emergency energy supply to homes, emergency response centers, hospitals, etc. Given Hawaii's commitment to transform its energy sector, and the unique value that such systems bring to Hawaii given its location, make it a prime candidate to develop resilient energy systems.

The search for solutions is helping fuel the growth of innovation in Hawaii. In fact, the very existence of isolated, islanded grids, along with the high energy costs and connections to the Asia-Pacific region has made Hawaii a uniquely attractive laboratory for clean energy solutions. Hawaii's strong commitment to clean energy, evidenced by progressive policies and high rates of deployment and integration has attracted entrepreneurs from around the world, looking to develop, test and prove emerging technologies and strategies before going to market, such as energy storage and smart inverters.

Yet, policy makers in Hawaii have been aware that the clean energy revolution, particularly the ability to install rooftop solar, has not taken place among all demographics and communities throughout the state. As a result, the Hawaii Legislature adopted a plan developed by the Hawaii Department of Business, Economic Development, and Tourism to combine securitized rate reduction bonds and on-bill repayment in the form of a green financing program that targets the underserved among residential customers, renters and nonprofits. This Green Energy Market Securitization (GEMS) program with its initial $150 million issuance of "AAA" bonds and roll-out of loan products has elicited international attention for its innovative approach to funding clean energy projects that can reach a broader clean energy market.

Hawaii's holistic view of its energy systems becomes even more attractive when considering the impact of removing carbon from the environment. The successful push for energy efficiency under the Hawaii Clean Energy Initiative is yielding unprecedented reductions in greenhouse gases. The State Energy Office estimates that at the current rate, the amount of CO_2 reductions will bring Hawaii into compliance with the state's greenhouse gas law well in advance of the

Mark Glick Testimony
U.S. Senate Committee on Energy and Natural Resources
Page 6
July 14, 2015

2020 requirement to meet 1990 CO2 levels. The analysis demonstrates that the 2020 emissions levels will be lower than the 1990 levels by approximately four percent based on conservative assumptions. Hawaii's efforts to reduce greenhouse gas emissions through a forward-looking energy policy has provided an option to employ a systems approach to carbon reduction that relieves the burden for all large emitters to develop reduction plans and strategies as long as the aggregate CO2 reduction levels are achieved, which should be of particular interest to anyone who lives on an island. With 750 miles of coastline in Hawaii, rising sea levels are a growing concern. Anything that can be done to mitigate greenhouse gas emissions will benefit the coastal communities in Hawaii, including iconic Waikiki Beach.

In conclusion, Hawaii has been able to leverage its isolation and the challenges faced in the arena of clean energy to great advantage. Hawaii has been able to attract international investment from governments and corporations that see Hawaii as a bellwether for renewable energy, and a place where the next generation of energy solutions will be born. This success prompted both the administration of Governor David Ige and the Hawaii Legislature to rethink the potential of Hawaii's clean energy transformation. The upshot was the passage of a bill -- signed by Governor Ige in June of this year -- calling for Hawaii's electric utilities to accelerate the 2020 interim RPS target for renewables from 25% to 30%. Hawaii's continual refinement of its RPS targets assists in resource optimization, prevents costly overbuilds, and sets a clear, unambiguous goal of generating one hundred percent (100%) of electricity sales from its renewable sources by 2045. Hawaii's approach of setting targets for its utilities is a practical approach to further the state's energy policies.

Thank you for this opportunity to highlight Hawaii's clean energy leadership and share some of the lessons we have learned in pursuing our clean energy transformation.

The CHAIRMAN. Mr. Hodge, welcome.

STATEMENT OF HUGO HODGE, JR., EXECUTIVE DIRECTOR/ CEO, VIRGIN ISLANDS WATER AND POWER AUTHORITY

Mr. HODGE. Good morning, Honorable Chairwoman Lisa Murkowski and other honorable members of the Committee on Energy and Natural Resources. My name is Hugo V. Hodge Jr., and I am the Executive Director/Chief Executive Officer of the Virgin Islands Water and Power Authority (VIWAPA). On behalf of the Governor of the Virgin Islands, the Honorable Kenneth E. Mapp, the Virgin Islands Delegate to Congress, the Honorable Stacey Plaskett, and the members of the 31st Legislature of the Virgin Islands, and the Governing Board of the VIWAPA, we thank you for this invitation.

To say that volatile oil prices have placed an undue burden on the businesses and residents of the U.S. Virgin Islands and the overall economy of the territory is an understatement. Since approximately 2003 when fuel oil prices began an unprecedented climb, electric customers have struggled to pay for electric services, spending approximately 9 percent of their income on these services versus the 2-percent paid by their mainland counterparts.

At one point in time, the average price of energy paid by the U.S. Virgin Islands consumer climbed to a high of $0.51 per kilowatt hour, five times the U.S. average. While the territory has received some relief in recent months due to the recent decline in oil prices which has reduced the current electric rate to $0.32 per kilowatt hour for residential customers and $0.35 per kilowatt hour for commercial customers, analysts are divided on how long this respite from high fuel prices will last. One thing is certain, however. Prices will elevate again, so the urgency remains the same.

Like most other Caribbean islands, the USVI has no conventional energy resources to meet its energy needs. While U.S. mainland utilities can connect to grids to purchase power from other utilities in the continental United States, island utilities are small, isolated, and are not interconnected to a grid comprised of other utilities. This is primarily due to their separation by water and the depth of the ocean floor, which makes interconnection via underwater electric cables technologically and economically unfeasible. As a result, island utilities have historically purchased small simple cycle generating units that are oil-fueled.

From the mid-1980's to approximately September 2003, the inflation-adjusted price of a barrel of crude oil on the NYMEX was generally under $25 a barrel. The attraction of low cost fuel, combined with the economies of scale, provided the framework for island utilities to purchase these small generating system. In many islands that are comprised of several small islands separated by water, duplicate generating systems and increased reserves are required to meet the need for electrical services. VIWAPA, for example, has two separate generating systems—one to serve the islands of St. Thomas, St. John, Water Island, and Hassel Island, and another separate system serves the island of St. Croix.

During 2003, oil prices globally began to steadily rise. The price per barrel paid for by the Authority was approximately $22 a barrel. At its highest, we have paid $141 per barrel. The result of these massive spikes caused operating cash shortfalls, flat to declining sales in electricity, and larger outstanding receivables, resulting in deferred maintenance on our generating equipment. I provide a table showing the rise of fuel prices.

So what we have done since that point is we have pursued every available option to reduce the cost of electric services to our customers and jump start the economy. We have pursued alternative and renewable sources tirelessly for almost 10 years now, and tangible relief is finally on the horizon. VIWAPA could not, however, have made the advances it has without a number of public and private partnerships.

Chief among our supporters have been the Department of Interior, the Department of Energy through its National Renewable Energy Laboratory, the Federal Emergency Management Agency, and the U.S. Department of Agriculture, and RUS, which have provided the following assistance. DOE through NREL helped to identify the territory's baseline energy use and how the USVI could best meet its goal to cut fossil fuels by 60 percent by 2025. VIWAPA, as an EDIN partner, has been able to tap into a broad spectrum of technical assistance and project development support from DOE and NREL. DOI provided a $500,000 grant for VIWAPA to prepare an Integrated Resource Plan that will provide the roadmap for responding to future generation needs. FEMA has provided funding for hazard mitigation projects that have assisted VIWAPA with burying power lines that serve areas critical to the territory's infrastructure. RUS has approved a loan that will allow VIWAPA to implement Distributed Automation Technology, a smart grid capital improvement project, and AMI, Advanced Metering Infrastructure. The closing on this loan has, however, been delayed. Any assistance the committee can provide to close the loan would be appreciated.

Throughout the rest of the testimony I highlight some of the things we have implemented. We were 100 percent dependent on fuel oil. Now we have about 8.2 megawatts of grid type solar and about 15 megawatts of net metering, bringing our renewable portfolio to just about 22, 23 percent currently. We also have another six megawatts of solar power we have contracted for to be built on the island of St. Croix. We have a seven-megawatt biofuel project on St. Croix contracted to be built by the end of 2016, and we are currently doing a massive undertaking of converting all of our power generation to use of LPG, or propane. The conversions of the units allow for both LNG and LPG, and we expect to see a significant reduction in costs as a result.

The Island of St. Croix will be benefiting from that project as early as next month. We plan to introduce propane to the storage facilities the end of July and produce energy in August. I am pleased to report that. The St. Thomas project is behind waiting for the issuance of an Army Corps of Engineer's permit, and we know they are doing their utmost to produce the permit. However, the permitting staff for the region, which reviews the permits, is inundated with other requests.

I would like to thank you for the opportunity to appear before the committee, and I am here to answer any questions you may have.

[The prepared statement of Mr. Hodge follows:]

HUGO V. HODGE, JR.
EXECUTIVE DIRECTOR/CEO
VIRGIN ISLANDS WATER and POWER AUTHORITY

STATEMENT BEFORE THE
COMMITTEE ON ENERGY AND NATURAL RESOURCES
UNITED STATES SENATE

HEARING ON

Remote and Isolated Energy Systems, Including Energy and Infrastructure
Challenges and Opportunities in Alaska, Hawaii and the U.S Virgin Islands.
JULY 13, 2015

Good day Honorable Chairperson Lisa Murkowski, and other honorable members of the Committee on Energy and Natural Resources. My name is Hugo V. Hodge Jr., and I am the Executive Director/Chief Executive Officer of the Virgin Islands Water and Power Authority (VIWAPA). In addition I am the chairperson of the Caribbean Electric Utilities Service Corporation (CARILEC) for the 2015-2016 term, and was recently selected to serve on the Board of Directors of the American Public Power Association (APPA). On behalf of the Governor of the Virgin Islands, the Honorable Kenneth E. Mapp, the Virgin Islands Delegate to Congress, the Honorable Stacey Plaskett, the members of the 31st Legislature of the Virgin Islands, and the Governing Board of the VIWAPA, we thank you for the invitation to provide testimony on the plight of remote and isolated energy systems.

SECTION 1. INTRODUCTION

To say that volatile oil prices have placed an undue burden on the businesses and residents of the US Virgin Islands and the overall economy of the Territory is an understatement. Since approximately 2003 when fuel oil prices began an unprecedented climb, electric customers have struggled to pay for electric services, spending approximately 9% of their income on these services verses the 2% paid by their mainland counterparts. At one point in time, the average price of electricity paid by U.S. Virgin Islands consumers climbed to a high of 50 cents per kilowatt-hour, five times the U.S. average. While the Territory has received some relief in recent months due to the recent decline in oil prices, which has reduced the current electric rate to 32 cent per kilowatt hour for residential customers, and 35 cents per kilowatt hour for commercial customers, analysts are divided on how long this respite from high fuel prices will last. One thing is certain however, prices will elevate again, and so the urgency remains the same.

Like most other Caribbean islands, the USVI has no conventional energy resources to meet its energy needs. While U.S. mainland utilities can connect to grids to purchase power from other utilities in the continental United States, island utilities are small, isolated and are not interconnected to a grid comprised of other utilities. This is primarily due to their separation by water and the depth of the ocean floor, which makes interconnection via underwater electric cables technologically and economically unfeasible. As a result, island utilities have historically purchased small simple-cycle generating units that are oil fueled. From the mid-1980s to approximately September of 2003, the inflation-adjusted price of a barrel of crude oil on the NYMEX was generally under $25/barrel. The attraction of low cost fuel combined with the economies of scale provided the framework for island utilities to purchase these small generation systems. In many islands that are comprised of several small islands separated by water, duplicate generation systems and increased reserves are required to meet the need for electrical services. VIWAPA for example has two separate generation systems. One system to serve the islands of St. Thomas, St. John, Water Island and Hassel Island and another separate system serves the island of St. Croix. The islands of St. Thomas and St. Croix are 36 miles apart and are not interconnected electrically due to the topography of the ocean floor.

During 2003, fuel oil prices globally began a steady rise. In 2003, the price per barrel of oil paid for by the Authority was approximately $22.00. At its highest, the VIWAPA paid $141.00 per barrel. The result of these massive spikes caused operating cash shortfalls, flat to declining electricity sales and larger outstanding receivables, resulting in deferred maintenance on VIWAPA's generating units.

The chart below demonstrates that while the amount of fuel that the Authority used for its operation has remained somewhat consistent over the years and has dropped in recent years, the price for fuel still remains high.

Figure 1 – Historical Fuel Purchase and Costs

Fuel Purchased	FY 04	FY 05	FY 06	FY 07	FY 08	FY 09	FY 10	FY 11	FY 12
Barrels-Mill	2.33	2.36	2.34	2.46	2.43	2.39	2.44	2.26	2.18
Paymts-$Mill	$76.80	$111.80	$149.20	$165.30	$214.60	$190.30	$184.60	$207.30	$264.60
Price Per Bbl	$32.96	$47.37	$63.76	$67.20	$87.23	$79.63	$75.66	$94.03	$121.33
Sales-GWh	741.2	763.8	767.5	776.4	775.9	724.3	754.8	755.8	723.9

Fuel Purchased	FY 13	FY 14	YTD (Apr 15)
Barrels-Mill	1.96	1.75	1.43
Paymts- Mill	$247.47	229.94	141.749
Price/bbl	128.94	131.23	94.72
Sales	680.5	641.04	518.5

SECTION 3. HOW VIWAPA IS REDUCING RATES

Since fuel prices began skyrocketing in 2003 VIWAPA has pursued every available option to reduce the cost of electric services to its customers and jump start the island economy. We have pursued alternative and renewable sources tirelessly for almost 10 years now, and tangible relief is finally on the horizon. VIWAPA could not, however, have made the advances that is has without a number of Strategic Public and Private Partnerships. Chief among our supporters has been the Department of Interior (DOI), the Department of Energy ~~thought~~ through its National Renewable Energy Laboratory (NREL), the Federal Emergency Management Agency (FEMA) and the US Department of Agriculture, Rural Utilities Services (RUS) which have provided the following assistance:

- DOE through NREL helped to identify the Territory's baseline energy use and how the USVI could best meets its goal to cut fossil fuel use by 60% by 2025.
- VIWAPA, as an EDIN project partner, has been able to tap into a broad spectrum of technical assistance and project development support from DOE and NREL,
- DOI provided a $500,000 grant for VIWAPA to prepare an Integrated Resource Plan (IRP) that will provide the road map for responding to future generation needs.
- FEMA has provided funding for hazard mitigation projects that have assisted VIWAPA with burying power lines that serve areas critical to the Territory's infrastructure.
- RUS has approved a loan that will allow VIWAPA to implement Distribution Automation Technology, a Smart Grid capital improvement project, and Advanced Metering Infrastructure and Automated Meter Reading (AMI/AMR). The closing on this loan has, however, been delayed. Any assistance the Committee can provide to close the loan would be appreciated.

Outlined below are the projects that VIWAPA has implemented, and is implementing, to reduce the cost of electric services to the Territory:

1. Until October of 2014, VIWAPA was 100% dependent on fuel oil to produce power. Since that time, VIWAPA has placed on its grid approximately 8.2 MW of solar power through partnerships with Toshiba International Corp, and Mainstreet Power Company/Morgan Stanley. The result is that approximately 8% of VIWAPA's peak demand generating capacity comes from renewable sources. The cost to the Authority to purchase power from these sources is $0.15 per kWh and $0.17 per kWh respectively.

2. In December of 2014, the Authority issued an RFP for 6 more MW of solar power on St. Croix and 3 more MW of power on St. Thomas. On January 22, 2015, the Authority signed contracts for 6MW of power with St. Croix Solar and St. Croix Solar II, project entities that were the result of a proposal that was submitted via competitive bid by a local St. Croix company, Caribbean Energy Opportunities in conjunction Foresight Renewable Solution a US Mainland Company. The purchase price is $0.13 per kWh. This project, barring unforeseen delays is anticipated to be in

commercial operation in fifteen months With regard to the 3 MW Solar Facility for St. Thomas, the Authority has selected a bidder and contract negotiations have been substantially completed. An executed Power Purchase Agreement (PPA) is anticipated in the upcoming months.

3. The Authority has entered into a contract with Tibbar Energy, USVI, LLC, ("Tibbar"), a qualified facility approved by the Virgin Islands Public Services Commission via the Territory's Cogeneration and Small Power Production Act at 30 VIC section 46 et. al. Tibbar will design, construct, and operate a king grass-fed anaerobic digester facility that generates biogas, which will be fed into generators that will produce up to 7 MW of power to sell to VIWAPA, at or below the Authority's avoided cost. Tibbar is anticipated to be in commercial operation by December, 2016.

4. VIWAPA in conjunction with the Virgin Islands Energy Office has completed wind studies to determine the economic feasibility of wind power development in the Territory. VIWAPA is currently in negotiations with several qualified facilities proposing wind projects that were approved by the Virgin Islands Public Services Commission pursuant to the Cogeneration and Small Power Production Act.

5. One of the pivotal actions taken by the V.I. Government to aide VIWAPA was the passage of Act 7360, which was signed into law on May 14, 2012. The Act established the Virgin Islands Water and Power Authority Generating Infrastructure Fund (the "Fund"). This Fund contains the proceeds from the gasoline tax which, pursuant to the same legislation, was increased from $0.07 to $0.14 per gallon. The money deposited into the Fund is to be used exclusively by the Authority to fund new energy efficient power generating units and/or heat recovery steam generators. This legislation is an instrumental piece of a larger plan to reduce the high cost of energy in the Territory, and will be the source, after the completion of the Integrated Resource Plan, to purchase the first new generation for the Authority in approximately 11 years.

6. Perhaps the largest, most-anticipated and ambitious project that VIWAPA is undertaking to bring relief to the businesses and residents is the conversion of its generating facilities to burn Liquefied Petroleum Gas (LPG) and Liquefied Natural Gas (LNG). VIWAPA has partnered with the VITOL Group, a Swiss-based, Dutch-owned multinational energy and commodity trading company, to supply lower cost and cleaner burning LPG for power generation, with an anticipated 30% reduction in fuel costs. VITOL, through its project entity, VITOL, Virgin Islands Corp., will: (1) construct, own, operate, and transfer the LPG facilities; (2) supply LPG and (3) manage the repowering of certain combustion turbine units.   To further the implementation of both the LNG and LPG projects, the combustion turbines (CTs) at VIWAPA's St. Croix and St. Thomas generating facilities are being converted to enable them to burn LPG and LNG in addition to fuel oil.

The project has not been without its challenges as there have been a number of unforeseen circumstances that have forced adjustments to the project completion schedules and cost, such as:

- Adverse weather conditions.
- Undocumented soil conditions and underground obstacles.
- Challenges in coordinating the conversion of the power plants to safely burn propane while simultaneously operating power generating facilities to meet daily electricity demand.
- Additional work required for the design, procurement and installation of the necessary resources to upgrade the existing fire protection, controls and systems for the safe use of propane.
- The complexity of permitting and the contracting, demolishing and disposing of structures with lead-based paint.
- The reality of global sourcing of all the materials and equipment for the project.
- Additional regulatory requirements to be complied with to assure the safety and the security of the marine aspect of the project, including necessary redesigns.

Notwithstanding the aforementioned challenges, the projects have realized many accomplishments to include:

- Fabrication and the delivery, from Belgium, of 18 propane storage tanks to the Virgin Islands. Eight (8) storage tanks have been installed on St. Croix and 10 storage tanks have been installed on St. Thomas.
- Building and commissioning new propane delivery vessels to deliver liquefied propane to WAPA's facilities.
- Implementation of advance navigation simulation with the VI Port Authority marine harbor pilots to ensure safe transit of LPG vessels into and out of WAPA docking facilities.
- Commencement of the conversion work on the turbines by GE.
- Completion of a comprehensive Fire and Risk Assessment and Hazardous Area Classification Study.
- Finalizing, with the assistance of the Virgin Islands Territorial Emergency Management Agency and the US Department of Homeland Security, an independent vulnerability assessment study to ensure compliance with local and federal mandates for safety and security to protect the well-being of the general public, employees, and first responders.
- Completion of engineering of electrical, instrumentation automation, process design, civil design, structural design, piping and mechanical design.
- Secured air and construction storm water permits for both facilities.
- Secured Coastal Zone Management Major Land and Water Permits for the development of the projects in both districts.
- Secured the U.S. Army Corps of Engineers (USACE) permit for the St Croix project. The St. Thomas permit is pending.
- Awaiting final approval of the Waterway Suitability Assessment (WSA) Plan, which focuses on the water side safety & security aspect of the projects, by the US Coast Guard.

I am pleased to report that the St. Croix Power Plant will be operating on LPG within the next 30 days. The St. Thomas project is, however, lagging behind. This is due to remaining work that is directly linked to the issuance of the US Army Corps of Engineers Permit, which the island of St. Thomas has not yet received. The USACE is doing its utmost to process the permit, however the permitting staff for the region which reviews the permits is inundated with other permit requests. Because of the critical need for this permit, any assistance this Honorable Committee can provide in this matter will be appreciated.

I would like to thank you for the opportunity to appear before the Committee today. I am happy to answer any questions that you may have.

The CHAIRMAN. Thank you, Mr. Hodge.
Welcome, Ms. Kohler.

STATEMENT OF MEERA KOHLER, PRESIDENT AND CEO, ALASKA VILLAGE ELECTRIC COOPERATIVE, INC.

Ms. KOHLER. Thank you. Good morning. My appreciation to Chairwoman Murkowski for inviting me here today and to all the members of the Committee for tolerating hearing a little bit about Alaska.

You have already had a brief introduction to AVEC, the Alaska Village Electric Coop. We are a non-profit electric utility that serves 56 communities, and we do so by operating 49 independent power plants. The reason we have to do that is because none of our communities are connected to each other, or very few of them are, although we have been on a mission for the last several years to try and interconnect our communities because that is how we can achieve economies of scale as well as allow us to integrate some wind power.

We actually are leaders in the development of wind power in Alaska. We own 34 wind turbines that serve 15 communities. We are able to achieve capacity reduction or diesel reduction of up to 30 percent in some of those communities, which is technologically a very challenging feat. Nonetheless, it is a mission that we do have to reduce our diesel consumption substantially.

I think, as was pointed out, the export of Alaskan dollars for fossil fuels is considerable. A very brief study that we did a few years ago shows that we are exporting $3 billion a year in fossil fuels used to power electricity and heat in our communities. We are, of course, an Arctic state, and as a result, heat is a very critical factor that has to be provided.

What we will find in Village Alaska and some of our smallest rural communities, over 20 percent of the population spends literally 50 percent or more of their disposal income on energy, and that is just electricity and heat. That is not supportable. You cannot have any type of economic development when you have energy that is crippling the economy.

Across the State of Alaska we have electric rates ranging from $0.10 a kilowatt hour in southeast Alaska where they have renewable hydro electricity up to over $1 a kilowatt hour in many of our communities where fuel has to be flown in. As Senator Murkowski mentioned, our river systems are changing. They are becoming shallower, and more and more communities are unable to be reached by barge traffic during the very brief summer season when we are ice free. So as a result, our challenges in Alaska truly are formidable.

These small local facilities do not have economies of scale because you are serving populations of just a few hundred. Our average village community in AVEC is 450, but if you look across the state where we have more than 200 microgrids as it were that are completely islanded, the average population in those villages really is more like 200. So when you are trying to develop a reliable energy system to serve such a small population, you actually wind up with a huge amount of redundancy.

We have typically three to four diesel generators in a village. They are sized such that they can pick up the loads during any one part of the season of the year. You have to be able to count upon having one generator down for planned maintenance and having another one break down unexpectedly, so you have to have at least triple redundancy in each of these communities.

As a result, our actual installed cost per service in our villages is five times or more that of the lower 48. So typically over here, the lower 48, you see a capital cost of about $2,500 per service. In our villages, it is more than $17,000 per village—per service. Those disparities result in very high non-fuel costs of power as well, so typically in one of our villages we are looking at over $0.60 per kilowatt hour for the first thousand kilowatt hours, as it were.

We must have affordable energy if we are going to have economic development. We must have jobs. We must be able to provide essential services. The State of Alaska has been a significant player. They have funded several programs to improve the cost of electricity. They have a renewable fund that has been in operation since 2008 and has plugged almost $300 million into developing renewable energy systems. They have innovative financing options for large-scale construction, they have a revolving Power Project Fund, and they have the power cost equalization to reduce the cost of residential electricity for the first 500 kilowatt hours, but Federal help is desperately needed in Alaska. We do not have a transmission grid. We would love to have a grid to be able to connect and disconnect to, so that is something that certainly should be on the plate in the future. The Energy Independence and Security Act has got the potential to be a huge player in Alaska, so we urge you to consider funding elements of that act so that we can have the Federal support that we need across Alaska.

With that, I stand ready to answer questions, and yield the floor back to Chairman Murkowski.

[The prepared statement of Ms. Kohler follows:]

Written Testimony
Submitted to the
United States Senate
Committee on Energy and Natural Resources

On

Micro-grids
July 14, 2015

Respectfully Submitted By Meera Kohler
President and CEO
Alaska Village Electric Cooperative, Inc.

Testimony of Meera Kohler
President and CEO, Alaska Village Electric Cooperative, Inc.
July 14, 2015

Chairman Murkowski, Ranking Member Cantwell, and Members of the Committee, thank you for the opportunity to testify on micro-grids in Alaska.

My name is Meera Kohler. I am the President and CEO of Alaska Village Electric Cooperative (AVEC), a position that I have held since 2000.

AVEC was established in 1967 as the culmination of an effort of the then-Governor of Alaska to find a way to deliver central station electricity to the small villages that housed Alaska's rural, mostly indigenous population. The task was daunting, given the distances, geography, absence of infrastructure of any kind and extreme climactic conditions of our great state.

Working with USDA REA (Rural Electrification Administration, now Rural Utilities Service) a unique electric cooperative was established – one that would serve communities whose physical boundaries did not coincide with those of other member villages. This patchwork of electric grids began with three communities that were electrified in late1968. Old Harbor, Nulato and Hooper Bay are an average of 400 air miles from Anchorage, AVEC's base of operations and an average of 470 miles from each other.

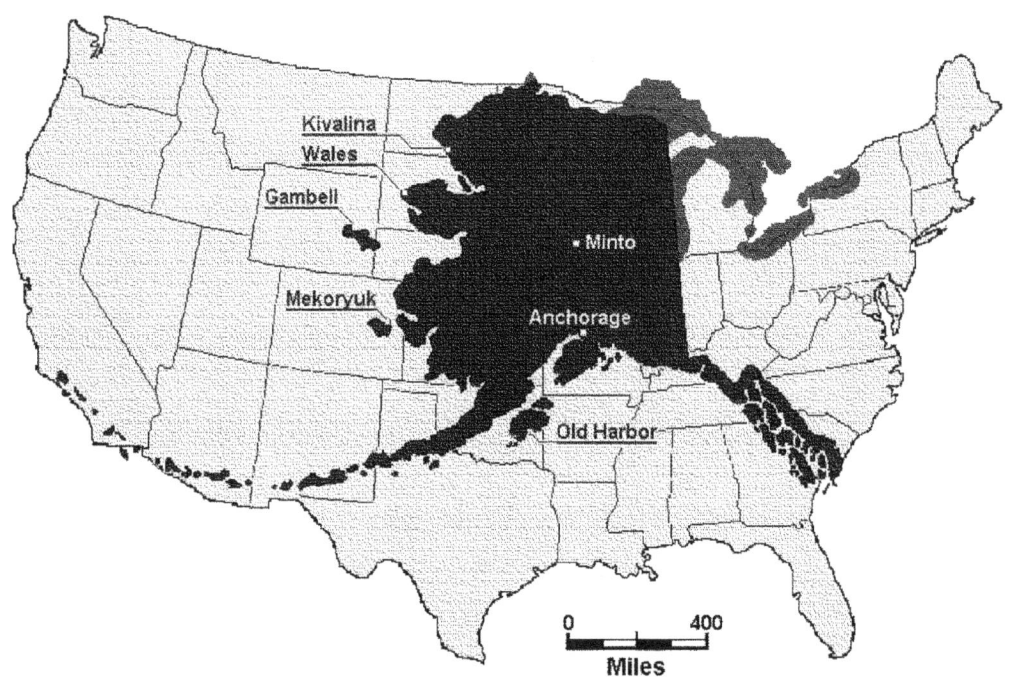

Testimony of Meera Kohler
President and CEO, Alaska Village Electric Cooperative, Inc.
July 14, 2015

AVEC today serves 56 communities in Alaska and does so with 49 separate diesel fueled power plants. Several of our communities have populations of less than 100 while our largest, Bethel, has a population of more than 6,200.

Discounting Bethel, which is more than five times the population of our second largest community, the average village population is 450 – likely less than the occupants of a single apartment building in most cities.

AVEC is, in effect, operating a series of 49 micro-grids. These micro-grids do not have the luxury of connecting or disconnecting to any other grid – as are virtually all communities and subsections of communities in the Lower-48. Instead we must provide redundancy within the community to allow for planned and unplanned generation maintenance. Extended outages in a community equate to life, health and safety crises almost immediately. During the winter, houses freeze up and human life is at risk. During the short summers, extended loss of refrigeration could mean the loss of an entire season of subsistence food.

AVEC systems typically consist of a stand-alone power plant with three or four generators. Sizing is carefully done so as to operate the most efficient generator to meet the needs of the day and the season. Redundancy is determined based upon having adequate capacity when the largest generator is down for maintenance and another fails unexpectedly. As a result, AVEC owns 80 megawatts of generation to supply an average load of 12 megawatts.

In addition to AVEC's 49 power plants, we maintain diesel tank farms in each community. Because fuel is delivered by barge during the short "open water" season, we must be able to store fuel for an entire year at a minimum. Since weather can delay the arrival of the first barge, we will generally ensure that we have up to 14 months of fuel on hand by the end of the delivery season.

In this day of the drive to distance ourselves from fossil fuels, rural Alaska's dependence on diesel is surprising to an outside observer. Alaska is one of the nation's leading energy states with vast reserves of natural gas. It would seem self-evident that Alaskans' energy needs would be met with inexpensive, low-emission sources such as that natural gas. That is not possible however, because Alaska lacks the basic infrastructure that is ubiquitous in other states.

Alaska lacks roads, railways, adequate port and dock facilities, paved runways, transmission grids, communication grids and other elements deemed necessary for modern American society. As a result, we have had to develop micro-systems to meet the needs of the people who have been resident in these areas for many hundreds of years. These micro-systems come at very high cost per capita.

Testimony of Meera Kohler
President and CEO, Alaska Village Electric Cooperative, Inc.
July 14, 2015

As an example, AVEC's investment in utility plant to serve our villages is more than $17,000 per service or meter. That is 4-5 times the investment typical in the Lower-48 and reflects the very large redundancy built into our generation system as well as the value of the fuel storage systems that go with it.

Despite these staggering costs, AVEC has nonetheless been a leader in deploying wind generation in communities with a robust wind regime. We typically install wind turbines that, at peak output, exceed the connected electrical load at the time. We install diversion systems that deflect excess wind generation to passive loads such as water boilers in water treatment plants and other public buildings and reduce the use of diesel fuel in those facilities.

AVEC has been engaged in developing wind generation since 2003 and owns and operates the largest fleet of wind turbines in Alaska – 34 machines are located in 11 communities and serve another four through modest transmission connections. We are able to achieve 25%+ of our generation from wind in communities with optimal wind regimes. In 2014, 6.4% of the electricity we sold came from wind. That is significantly better than the US total of 4.4%.

AVEC has also branched out into the tug and barge business. With diesel fuel playing a critical role in meeting the energy needs of rural Alaska, AVEC decided to enter this arena in order to deliver lower cost fuel to its constituents. The vessels were constructed in 2011 and have consistently lowered the cost of fuel transportation across the entire western Alaska market.

Alaskans do not wish to be tied to the yoke of fossil fuels, and especially diesel. Fuel spills occur routinely because the fuel is stored and handled so frequently, although rarely are they of such magnitude as to command national attention. Nonetheless, they are a continuing threat to human health and extremely expensive to respond to. That is why AVEC is committed to reducing our dependence on diesel fuel, which can only be achieved by improving efficiencies and by installing alternative sources of generation.

Efficiencies are achieved through optimizing generator output and to using the largest generator practical since efficiencies improve with generator size. We have been interconnecting communities as practical with a view toward optimizing generation efficiency and spreading the benefits of wind.

The cost of operating a power plant accounts for almost nine cents a kWh. That is the average cost of a kWh in the Lower-48 today – but is only one sixth of the cost of a kWh across our system. The chart below depicts the cost components of an AVEC kWh in 2014.

Testimony of Meera Kohler
President and CEO, Alaska Village Electric Cooperative, Inc.
July 14, 2015

Fuel	32.45
Power Production	8.78
Admin and General	3.15
Depreciation	2.91
Consumer Accounts	1.73
Distribution	1.19
Interest	1.14
Taxes	0.47
Margins	2.87
Total	54.69

Because of the very poor economies of scale in rural Alaska, costs are very high. Each stand-alone generation and distribution system account for 1.5 full time equivalent employees and two local part time employees to operate the plant. All technical, administrative and support services are provided from our Anchorage headquarters.

To put the very small scale of these utility operations into perspective, a village's entire annual kWh consumption is the equivalent of half the consumption of a grocery store in Anchorage. All 56 of our communities together represent a population of almost 32,000, about the same as Fairbanks, but the combined electrical usage is less than 10% of Fairbanks.

Electricity is the underpinning of modern society. Without abundant, affordable, reliable electricity, modern society cannot function efficiently. That is palpable in rural Alaska and, to a lesser extent, in urban Alaska as well, where the cost of electricity is 150% that of the US average.

As we address the delivery of electricity, AVEC is keenly attuned to the interlinked needs of sustainability for our communities. Space heat is typically provided by diesel fuel as well as electricity. Again, cost-effective alternatives are simply not available or practical. Transportation infrastructure in and to our communities is almost non-existent. Economic development is stymied absent these underlying basic needs and the social fabric of the community is strained by the day-to-day struggle of existence.

Testimony of Meera Kohler
President and CEO, Alaska Village Electric Cooperative, Inc.
July 14, 2015

The State of Alaska has been a major player in the effort to overcome the shortfall in infrastructure to serve Alaska – a role that in the Lower-48 was largely met by the federal government. The Denali Commission has been a significant contributor when funding was available in past years. Unfortunately, their role has perforce diminished as funding sources have dwindled.

It is time for a renewed, holistic approach to meeting the basic infrastructure needs of rural Alaska. With the US chairmanship of the Arctic Council, a spotlight is being shone on the US' only arctic state – Alaska. This is where the impacts of climate change are being most sharply felt. This is where economic and living conditions most closely resemble those of developing countries. This is where the vast resources of the Arctic Ocean nurture the land and the people and whose shores will witness the evolution of new transportation, tourism and mineral extraction activities.

It is time for the federal government to partner with the State of Alaska and those of us that exist to serve Alaskans to continue and enhance the infrastructure development that is critical for our future.

In the energy sector, the State has established the Power Cost Equalization program to make a lifeline amount of electricity affordable for individual Alaskans, while non-residential users pay unaffordable electric and heat bills to operate their modest businesses. The State has established a Renewable Energy funding program that has been better capitalized than any other state. Millions of gallon of diesel are being displaced annually by projects funded by this program. The State has established low cost financing options for energy infrastructure for larger utilities. The State funds research opportunities for emerging energy technologies.

But the State cannot carry all of the necessary infrastructure development with its limited resources. I plead with you as you consider a comprehensive energy bill that you include revisions to USDOE's loan program that is currently geared toward "innovative non-commercial" technologies. It should be looking instead at deploying innovative commercially viable technologies, such as what we are trying to do on a small scale.

Besides the federal government providing more assistance for transmission in rural areas to make micro-grid systems more economically efficient, it should also provide additional aid to help reduce the currently relatively high capital costs of renewable energy system installation. While renewables in high-cost, typically micro-grid systems, may save on operating costs, their high capital costs make financing them exceptionally difficult, given their high per customer installation costs. Wind, solar, biomass/pellet fuel, hydro and hopefully marine hydrokinetic systems in the future may all provide lower cost alternatives for generation compared to fossil fuels, but their initial capital costs make financing them exceptionally difficult in most micro-grid areas.

The federal government has passed legislation to help with these costs. The Department of Agriculture runs the High Energy Cost Grant program through the Rural Utility Service (RUS) that does make grants, plus loans, available to fund the installation of renewable electricity systems, but funding for the program has been cut repeatedly over the past decade. And Congress in 2007 approved in the Energy Independence and Security Act the creation of two matching grant programs to provide grants for up to 50% of the cost of installing proven renewable energy systems in high-cost regions. Unfortunately those grant programs have never been implemented by the Department of Energy nor actually been funded by the executive and legislative branches. Providing additional funding for these programs, plus for additional transmission aid, also currently available through RUS, would dramatically improve the likelihood that islanded grids could afford to install renewable energy systems and not only reduce consumer power costs over time, but also reduce the consumption of fossil fuels with their associated emissions.

We should be expanding our vision of micro-grids to include sustainable clusters of communities that are not connected to a grid but that collectively can be served by robust technologies that represent reliable, affordable, clean abundant energy.

Thank you for the opportunity to testify.

The CHAIRMAN. Thank you, Meera. I appreciate you being here and for your testimony this morning.

I have several questions this morning. Let me start with you first, Assistant Secretary. Under the Omnibus Appropriations bill from 2015, the Secretary of the Interior was directed to establish energy action plans for the territories which you mentioned in your comments. It also included Puerto Rico, but Puerto Rico is not yet included in the process. Where are we with Puerto Rico's inclusion?

Obviously Puerto Rico is clearly and keenly in the news right now. We are all very engaged in these issues that are very, very difficult for Puerto Rico. I have noted that as difficult as the economy is right now, unless we can deliver and work with the people of Puerto Rico on some energy solutions, it is going to continue to be a tough set of facts there. So where are we on the energy action plan for Puerto Rico?

Ms. KIA'AINA. Thank you, Chairwoman, for that question. When the law was passed, our Fiscal Year 2015 budget did not take into account Puerto Rico, so the $3 million that we received went to other areas in the other territories. As I stated in my testimony, the plan estimated by NREL will cost $330,000. We believe that if we received our full funding for Fiscal Year 2016, which is $4.4 million, we would be able to accommodate Puerto Rico in the upcoming Fiscal Year.

The CHAIRMAN. So to this point in time, there has been nothing done to pursue an energy action plan for Puerto Rico. Is that correct?

Ms. KIA'AINA. That is correct; however, there is NREL and there is the U.S. Department of Energy. I have been in contact with the U.S. Department of Energy, and they actually have told me that a plan may not be necessary because they have already done a lot of work in Puerto Rico. So I commit to you after this hearing—well, first, let me just say for Fiscal Year 2016, we can fund it if we get an increase in appropriation.

With regard to what can DOI and U.S. DOE do now, I need to followup with my colleague at the Department of Energy, who is already active in Hawaii and the Virgin Islands and has said that a lot of ground work has been made in Puerto Rico. And so, they may have the discretionary authority to do that plan. That is something I will followup with your staff as well as with the Department of Energy.

The CHAIRMAN. I would appreciate you doing that. We had invited representatives from NREL or DOE to attend this morning to speak to some of these issues, so hopefully they are on alert that these are questions that we would like to have addressed. I am sure that the people of Puerto Rico would like to know that there is a plan that is out there.

Nobody has really talked this morning about storage capacity, and I know that for the areas that you all represent and are engaged in, the ability to store energy from these intermittent sources is really going to be the future here. What level of engagement have you had with the Department of Energy on these microgrid technologies that you are working on to improve storage capacity? Has there been much work either in Alaska, Hawaii, or the territories? Mr. Glick?

Mr. GLICK. Chairman Murkowski, the Department of Energy has provided a great deal of technical assistance through some of the analyses that we talked about. The Oahu wind integration study, as well as the solar integration study did talk about amounts of storage that would be necessary to smooth out frequency disruptions and other technical problems created through intermittent power. So there have been RFPs that have been put together by the utility to solicit that amount of storage for our systems, but we also believe that it is important to do grid modernization, which will relieve a lot of demand for storage through these trip inverters and other technologies I discussed, which are a lot less expensive. So we have to do both.

The CHAIRMAN. Mr. Hodge?

Mr. HODGE. Yes, good morning again. We have been talking to the Department of Energy about a microgrid system for the island of St. John. It is an isolated part of our grid, it is served by underwater submarine cables, it is about eight megawatts in total, and we believe that the island is ideal for a microgrid system with distributed generation and storage. We have asked for their assistance, and I believe we are just about close to getting some technical assistance in studying how we can do our microgrid system for that island.

We also look at other mechanisms for our utilities scale. Solar, we use some of the European standards, the low voltage ride through, the frequency support, and some of the other technologies that are in the inverters that are not predominant in the U.S. markets, but that are more prevalent in the other countries that utilize the renewables.

The CHAIRMAN. Let us go to Senator Cantwell.

Senator CANTWELL. Thank you, Madam Chair. The Napaskiak. Is that where we——

The CHAIRMAN. That is where we were.

Senator CANTWELL. So Senator Murkowski and I were at Napaskiak two summers ago. Ms. Kohler, one of the things that you said that struck me is this nexus between economic development—energy costs and economic development. You are not going to grow an economy if you do not have basic energy costs that are competitive for people to establish businesses there. So this is, to me, a very critical issue. One of the things I mentioned in my statement was about the two challenges that we have, both the technical barriers on the ground and in the workforce and then the financial investments or the structure to deploy that.

Of the programs that we currently operate at the Federal level, what are the holes? Why does this not work to try to test or deploy other technologies, or maybe you think they are working fine?

Ms. KOHLER. Well, I would like to say they are working fine, but the reality of the matter is that when you are looking at—you mentioned Napaskiak, and that is a standalone community that operates their own electric system. When you are that small you do not have access to technical resources that you can afford, and so you rely upon other entities, such as the State of Alaska through the Alaska Energy Authority, for assistance.

Now, on the other hand, in our communities, the AVEC communities, because we are headquartered in a single location, we have the technical staff and the engineering resources and so forth to provide the support services we need for our own communities. You still have a real issue with local capacity. When we install wind turbines, for example, in our communities, we actually send individuals that are residents in those communities, typically one or two people, to extensive wind training so that they actually become wind smiths, as it were. They are supported by journeymen level staff out of our own office, but it makes for very expensive alternatives.

U.S. DOE has not really played a major part, but the Denali Commission has been a very strong supporter and has provided funding for renewables and for training as part of the operation of those renewables. I know that very recently the Alaska Center for Energy and Power is working with U.S. DOE to put together a modest innovative program to develop storage alternatives.

The storage that we use to operate our wind turbines really is a diversion off that excess electricity into heat sources. We actually use the electricity as heat to supplant diesel in public projects, water treatment plants and so forth. So we do effectively use it, although the best value for that electricity would be as electricity. But until storage becomes more of a mainstream event, as it were, we cannot afford to invest in it.

Senator CANTWELL. So financing really is an issue.

Ms. KOHLER. Financing is the hugest issue of all, yes.

Senator CANTWELL. And that seems to me to be the crux of this—I am not saying the complexity of Alaska and its temperature is not a very challenging issue, but it does not seem to me that these problems are about getting a national lab to tell us what we need to do here. It is more about whether the tools are there for the communities to build capacity that they do not have to begin with because of remoteness or the lack of a business interest. It seems to me that the financial tools that we are making available seems to be a very critical issue. You are nodding your head. You agree?

Ms. KOHLER. I am agreeing with you 100 percent.

Senator CANTWELL. Okay. Mr. Underwood, Mr. Glick, or Mr. Hodge?

Congressman UNDERWOOD. Yes, that is exactly it. I think the main issue we are—and certainly in small island societies, you are waiting for some technological innovation to come along to solve your problem instead of—and what happens is that the shifting of the responsibility of, well, how do you finance some of these things, and how do you finance innovations and adopt them into your island society that has shifted. It shifted to other places, and you are just kind of waiting for something to happen. I would argue that and I would urge that Federal agencies spend as much time giving some island communities as much technical assistance on how to finance things as much as technological advice or advice on new techniques.

Also, just to speak briefly to the point about storage. That is also a very critical issue, and I am eager to hear what the others have done with this issue because the inability to store from solar panels is one of the biggest reasons why some people argue you should not adopt solar panels now until you get that level of technology. I just—I do not accept that. I think there must be ways of managing that grid and power consumption throughout the day in order to manage that, so that storage issue.

But just to speak briefly again to the issue of technical assistance, and financing, and developing models for that is really as much a key as is advice on new technologies.

Senator CANTWELL. Well, I am a big—oh, Mr. Hodge, did you want to say something?

Mr. HODGE. Yes. I would like to say that having the utility be a part of the plan is critical because how we have tackled the issues of financing is by using the PPA model. So where the utility or the government could not outright finance the project or do the borrowing for the project, our utility can use a mechanism called a power purchase agreement to pledge the repayment over a period of time via the rates for that reduction in cost.

For our LPG conversion, we had a worldwide company, VITOL, put up all of the upfront costs, the $150 million, the conversion, of all of our units, all the facility, build all the infrastructure. And then over a period of just 10 years, we can repay this debt via a small add-on to our cost of buying the propane from the Gulf, so it is U.S. fuel. And the PPA model we have used for our solar projects with 25-year PPAs. We have got $0.13, $0.14 for solar energy on a utility scale. We have utilized it for our bio fuel project.

We do not have the capital to go out and do large purchases or utility-owned systems, but by using the PPA model, which does require that you maintain investment-grade, which is a challenge for some utilities but that is the way we handle that issue.

Senator CANTWELL. Well, I was going to say I am a big fan of public power in general, and we had one utility in our area, Parkland, which is in Pierce County, that basically put all its utilities underground. So here is a little utility that decided what was in the best interest of those rate payers was an investment in securing their delivery system because of our winds and storms. They decided to finance that and move ahead.

So I like having the public models in the marketplace, because I think that they keep a keen eye on the interest of cost-based power in delivering the resource to the community that allows the community to grow. While I am a very big supporter of Power Africa in the context of the United States doing all it can to take U.S. technology and promote it in other areas, it is an embarrassment that we are not spending more time and energy in the United States of America and our territories providing real solutions to the people that live within our boundaries. We have got to do this.

Madam Chair, I am all ears about the solutions that we can seek to do this. This is something that we should do, and it should be a commitment by this government to get it done. Thank you.

The CHAIRMAN. Well, you are singing to the choir here. [Laughter.] Let us have Senator Hirono join.

Senator HIRONO. Thank you very much, Madam Chair, and I echo those sentiments about singing to the choir.

I am a proponent of the setting of national renewable energy and efficiency standards to encourage the private sector to step forward with R&D. Mr. Glick, I note in your testimony that you say that Hawaii has been able to attract international investment from governments and corporations. They see Hawaii as a bellwether for renewable energy. So I wanted to have you talk a little bit more about how Hawaii has spurred this kind of activity on the part of the private sector.

Mr. GLICK. For us, clean energy, as you know, Senator Hirono, has been all about rebuilding our economy and creating this new clean energy sector. Part of it is attracting innovation. With us in Hawaii as being an emerging test bed, companies like Hitachi with support from the Ministry of Economy and Trade and Industry in Japan have been funneling dollars. About $40 million came to Maui for the smart grid project called Great Maui that is building a microgrid and a smart grid network—also developing bigger networks of electric vehicles and fast charging networks. A very important project which we expect will expand.

Through the Hawaii-Okinawa Agreement which was just signed last week, we are hoping to identify additional projects that could be brought to Hawaii and also shared resources, some that would be developed in Japan as well. I think that is the kind of model that we see in the future continuing to find collaborative projects to test the boundaries of how we integrate more renewables, how do we build smarter clean transportation systems using clean energy, and trying to track those dollars on very large-scale real world demonstrations.

Senator HIRONO. We have heard from some of the other witnesses how expensive energy is in their localities. So, again, Mr. Glick, Hawaii created the Green Energy Market Securitization Program, or GEMS, to help more people invest in renewable energy. This is particularly important to people who do not have the money up front to buy solar panels, for example, but who are interested in saving money in the long term by generating their own power. Can you elaborate on how the GEMS Program works in engaging with the public and providing financing options to people, including renters and non-profit organizations, and do you think this approach could be used in other territories and other states?

Mr. GLICK. Thank you, Senator Hirono. Certainly the GEMS approach, we use rate reduction bonds that are securitized. They are backed in our case by security from the Public Benefits Fund, which comes from everybody's electricity bill, a small surcharge. We are able to utilize some of that back, repay the loans. We are able to get triple A financing, so very, very low cost of money.

We then build loan programs around it. It is hard getting small commercial non-profit organizations and also the residential market. Those loan products have just been rolled out this summer, and we expect a lot of people to take advantage of that. Very low interest rates on the low side, five to six percent, on the high side, nine percent. But compared to other programs, particularly for those who have had difficulty getting financing for solar projects, it is really the only way that they have been able to get financing.

And then, of course, tying it to your electricity bill repayment really reduces the risk of default, so I think that is another thing that can be incorporated. I know many states have had difficulty getting on bill programs instituted, and that is done pretty much on state-by-state level so far. But on bill does reduce risk of repayment, so we see that as an important model.

As far as the overall capitalization and how bond programs like GEMS could be expanded, we know that the State Energy Program through states and the state energy offices have managed $2.1 billion in loans. Perhaps the State Energy Program through some kind of mechanism like GEMS could funnel additional dollars. In Hawaii, we think our clean energy installations will exceed $20 billion in capitalization, so we need to find more means of financing to make it more affordable.

Senator HIRONO. Madam Chair, it seems as though my time is up, although it did not feel like five minutes. Is this right? Do you mind if I just ask Ms. Kia'aina whether a GEMS kind of a model could work in the other areas, territories?

Ms. KIA'AINA. I think some of my other colleagues in the territories might be better able to answer that question, but just let me say in general our energy program is so small, $3 million. So I would promote greater dialog with the private sector, and I took notice of Hitachi, Mr. Glick, because in the Pacific territories, Japan is a close neighbor. They have committed $450 million just recently for climate change and other types of funding specifically for independent Pacific Island nations, including Micronesia. And so, my head was thinking here with regard to some Kokua we could use for our energy initiatives.

That is something we will contemplate, but, again, I defer to my other colleagues directly from the territories because they are on the front lines, and they are probably already working with the private sector.

Senator HIRONO. If it is all right with the chair, if anybody else wants to chime in.

Congressman UNDERWOOD. Yes, I think that is a—that is a possibility, and it goes back to the whole point about how to finance these things in the small island territories. I think there is kind of a common perception that OIA is going to fund some of this, or that they are going to create some kind of financing mechanism. But it is not there, and we recognize that. At least I recognize that. I am not sure that everyone does.

But this is the kind of promising thing that I think could come from an all-islands approach where we are constantly having these dialogs. I should not have to go to Washington, DC. to hear about it when I can just go to Honolulu. [Laughter.]

Senator HIRANO. Mr. Hodge.

Mr. HODGE. Yes, we have used on bill financing for our solar water heater program, so I am sure somewhat the model can work. I am not familiar with the GEMS Program and what the surcharge is on a per kilowatt hour basis that is used to backstop the financing or the debt, and I guess it would be also dependent on the scale and size of the billing. So if you have two million customers, a small surcharge would be much different with 50,000 customers to backstop that kind of an endeavor. But I will do some more research to see if it is applicable for our small territory.

Senator HIRONO. Thank you. Did you want to add something?

Ms. KOHLER. If I could just add, there really is not a lot of private party interest in providing or looking for solutions for our small villages because the economies of scale again are so poor. The average village sells, you know, 1.3 million kilowatt hours. There is just not enough to be able to amortize an investment of any size, so I do not really see that it would have a lot of potential application for our villages.

Senator HIRONO. I think you definitely have a very unique situation, and that is why you have a wonderful senator who is going to address some of those needs. Thank you very much, Madam Chair.

The CHAIRMAN. Thank you. I think it is valuable when we have hearings such as this for us not only to hear the different projects and proposals that are underway and the challenges, but how you are facing those, and to share a little bit of best practices. I would agree with you, Mr. Underwood. You should not have to come all the way to Washington, DC. to find these, but hopefully we gain from one another as we try to find these solutions that are oftentimes very unique.

But then you think not necessarily so. Just because it is perhaps colder and darker in Alaska when you are trying to make application to an area that is so isolated, and remote, and small, there are applications not only with our territories, but I think about the value of what we are doing in Alaska and sharing it with other Arctic nations who are also dealing with cold, and remote, and small populations. Again, sharing some of these best practices that are innovative to where we are.

You mentioned, Ms. Kohler, the triple redundancy that we face in Alaska and the need to have the backup generating capacity because if you are not part of anybody's else's grid when power goes out, power goes out. If you are in a cold place, if it goes out for a period of time, not only do you face the loss of your infrastructure through broken pipes and damage, but you could face loss of life. So for us, it is pretty critical.

I am just curious with the other systems that we are talking about whether it is in Guam or in our Caribbean islands, are you also in a situation where it is effectively triple redundancy for your backup generation capacity?

Mr. HODGE. Yes, ma'am, it is, and——

The CHAIRMAN. Tell me how that adds then to the cost to your rate payers.

Mr. HODGE. We have to have that redundancy in our generation. We use the N-minus-one criteria, so we have to be able to serve all of our load if our two largest units are offline, and you have to have that kind of criteria given that you have no interconnection with the grid.

We are doing a conversion right now to LPG, and we are converting units one at a time. Because there is no grid, we are doing that while we are still trying to meet the N-minus-one criteria, which is even that much more challenging to make change and to affect change. We have not even discussed the water side of it, because there are some synergies between water and electricity that I know that everyone kind of gets into on a regular basis.

But definitely there are reliability requirements on an island grid, and we do collaborate. I think there is an island and a grid in Alaska called Kodiak, Alaska that I have spent some time speaking with their wind—that they have put out a grid through DOE and NREL. They put us together since we have some similar characteristics, so there are some synergies between the territories and the State of Alaska as well.

The CHAIRMAN. Mr. Underwood?

Congressman UNDERWOOD. Yes. I cannot say that I do not know whether we have double or triple redundancy, but we do have redundancy because the—and we also have issues with resiliency in connection with our natural disasters. That really leaves a great deal of challenges to the power companies.

But part of that is, again, an issue of energy literacy, people understanding that and then people changing their habits on how the use power throughout the day so that you do not need that level of redundancy. So, you know, we have a smart grid, you also need smart people in order to use those grids, and that speaks to the issue of capacity building and energy literacy, which, of course, speaking as an educator, I am really trying to present to all the authorities and policymakers on that.

The CHAIRMAN. Senator Cantwell?

Senator CANTWELL. Thank you, Madam Chair. Ms. Kia'aina, this issue of financing or just where we are with current programs and gaps, you obviously see this issue from the perspective of the assistance provider, and you see what these individuals are requesting. You know what we can and cannot do. Do you have specific ideas about what you think we should do to improve that?

Ms. KIA'AINA. Well, the easiest answer, of course, is for our energy program of $3 million, it would be nice to see an increase not only just to help in the implementation of all of the energy plans, but to take into account Puerto Rico.

Apart from our direct funding for energy initiatives, we actually tap from our other programs right now maintenance assistance, which is only a $1 million program. We provide technical expertise, apprenticeship programs and staff training. We also take money from our general technical assistance program, as well as our capital improvement projects. So what we are doing is pulling from other areas that are already stretched thin.

I would also say that with regard to the Department of Energy's involvement, whether it be the energy as a whole or NREL, if there is increased funding to that Department, I ask that it specifically by designated for the U.S. territories and Puerto Rico because very often other agencies put it in the national pot, and the territories are unable to compete. The Office of Insular Affairs is one of the only unique programs in the Federal Executive Branch that actually has the territories competing for a set pot of funding.

So absolutely increased funding would help. I believe that our energy program is the best return on investment for our entire program, and helping the islands will not just help in energy, but the totality of their economy.

Senator CANTWELL. On this point about empowering them to help secure financing, do you see solutions in these individual territories or states that you think are just a matter of whether they can be deployed?

Ms. KIA'AINA. You know, that is a very difficult question to answer because our mission is the overall Federal relationship with the territories. So while we are talking about energy, I believe that our government's failure to help in the overall economic conditions of each of the insular areas would be hurtful to energy initiatives because they are all intertwined. For example, if a government does not have enough revenues to fund its portion of energy initiatives, then the burden will transfer to the Federal Government. So for my role, I have a dual purpose. I not only help on energy initiatives, but I help on the overall front on a multitude: health, education.

Senator CANTWELL. Which I think to your point then, says you are uniquely qualified. I do not know if you have quantified that in a study, the analysis of the lack of investment in energy, then the consequences, cost, and expense to the U.S. Government because we do not.

Ms. KIA'AINA. That is correct.

Senator CANTWELL. So if you have any data on that, we would love to see it.

Ms. KIA'AINA. Thank you so much. We will followup with that, Senator.

Senator CANTWELL. I did not mean to cut you off, but I had forgotten that your position was so broad. You were covering the consequences of lack of investment as well, so, if there was anything you wanted to add about how we should look at financing?

Ms. KIA'AINA. Financing for me is making the territorial governments efficient so that they could derive enough revenues to help with funding their local government. It is promoting economic opportunity so that their private sector could also help. Part of our mission is also quality of life issues to ensure that the health, education, and natural resources are protected.

Our mission at OIA is formidable. We work across the Executive Branch with other agencies, but part of the challenge, quite frankly, is that we always get the answer from every agency that if we do not provide funding, whether it be for travel, or for detailees, or for money to do studies, for example, GDP. We have to give the Department of Commerce money to do GDP.

So in short, the OIA is being used as a funding source for what the Federal Government in its totality should be doing. I myself believe it is unfair. Some of it is statutory in nature. It is only inclusive of the 50 states, and sometimes it is not. It is the agencies that are telling us they will not do this until we give them money. The GDP numbers, for example, in the totality of the economy is nearly $1 million, and that pot is taken out of our $50 million Technical Assistance Program, and that is money that could be used for energy initiatives.

Senator CANTWELL. Thank you for that illumination. I am not sure I wanted to hear that, but nevertheless, I am glad to understand it. Just mark me down as somebody who believes in flat organizational structures. I think that an information age is about empowering people at the lowest level, not a hierarchy bureaucracy all the way from Washington, DC. trying to tell somebody how to implement solutions. That is not going to work. I think we see that in Puerto Rico at the moment, and it is not going to be successful. So I think we need to rethink some of these issues. Thank you.

Ms. KIA'AINA. Thank you.

The CHAIRMAN. Senator Hirono?

Senator HIRONO. Thank you, Madam Chair. Ms. Kia'aina, I am glad that you mentioned our country's responsibility to do more to invest in the territories and to help create more economic opportunities there, because it is all interconnected. I know that your mission also incorporates the concerns under the compact of free association. Since that has been brought up, I did want to make the point that I do not think that our country is meeting its obligations under our compacts, and that this is something that the State of Hawaii as well as Guam and other impacted states because of these compacts, that we need to do a lot more to provide resources to states such as Hawaii, and places such as Guam, Arkansas probably.

The impact of compact migrants in our states is large, and we do not provide enough resources to help a state like Hawaii, as I mentioned, to meet our country's obligations toward our compact migrants. So I did want to take the time to mention that.

While I have you, Ms. Kia'aina, has the Department of Interior applied any of the lessons that were learned from DOE's planning and technical assistance in developing the Hawaii Clean Energy Initiative in Interior's efforts to assist the U.S. territories in their energy planning efforts? Perhaps you could talk a little bit about those lessons learned that enabled you to work with the territories?

Ms. KIA'AINA. Sure. If you do not mind, I would like to defer that question to our NREL liaison. NREL falls under the Department of Energy, and so our whole direction for our energy planning process is provided by NREL. Recently we have reached out directly to the U.S. Department of Energy because they also have their own resources. They have an Office of Energy Efficiency, and that was the division that I spoke to with regard to the chairwoman. There seems to be a disconnect right now with regard to what the Department has done for Puerto Rico, and we will followup on that.

Scott, could you please answer that question?

Mr. HAASE: Thank you. Scott Haase. I am a senior program manager with the National Renewable Energy Laboratory, and I manage our relationship with the Department of the Interior.

So the team that worked on the HCI, EDIN, and the territorial work, we all work together. It is many of the same people that have been working across these island communities. So there have been significant lessons learned that have carried forward throughout from technical assistance, the planning side, looking at financing options and mechanisms. So, yes, there has been a great deal of cross-fertilization.

Senator HIRONO. Well, Mr. Hodge, I note that the Virgin Islands have been able to meet its energy reduction goals much more quickly than anticipated. In 2011 you had a goal of 60 percent reduction of fossil fuel, and by 2013 you had already reached a 20 percent reduction. How did you do that?

Mr. HODGE. We aggressively sought for diversification of our resources. We issued some RFPs for renewable energy, and the first one was a broad RFP for any kind of technology. That one was failed, so we found that more concentrated requests would be better served for our needs. So we did one for solar, and we received some really good bids. We had assistance from NREL and DOE in the evaluation of such, and we received eight megawatts of grid-tied solar on the grid right now from that process, and six more soon to come.

We also had an aggressive net metering program. I cannot say that I think all aspects of the program are in the best interest of all rate payers, but it has served the purpose of jump starting the program. And we do have about 50 megawatts of net metering on the grid right now, so between both of them we are 23 percent of our peak demand. So those two have done that, but we also have, like I said, six megawatts of solar in the wings that have already been signed, PPAs, and seven megawatts of biofuel that have been signed, as well as we are negotiating about seven to ten megawatts of wind. So we are pretty much on the right path of getting to our goals.

Part of the 60 percent is energy efficiency, and we have done some advances in that arena as well. We definitely—you know, I guess being that I sit on some positions in the region in the Caribbean and whatnot, I see a lot of studies and a lot of examinations of what can be done. To finally have somewhere and it be ours that have the actual projects built, shoveling dirt, construction on the way, and almost complete is something that we need to see more of rather than just the studies of what we can do, and spend a lot of money for those studies.

Senator HIRONO. Yes, hear, hear. Thank you, Madam Chair.

The CHAIRMAN. Ms. Kohler, we talk a lot about the price of energy, and we talk about per kilowatt hour, but we also have the issue of heating. Can you speak to what you see as perhaps some of the more innovative approaches to how we can deal with space heat and the ways that the cost of space heating can be brought down in some of the villages that are part of your oversight with AVEC?

Ms. KOHLER. Thank you, Chairwoman Murkowski. Space heat is the primary consumer of BTUs at this particular point in time and typically represents about three-quarters of the energy consumption in a home or a business. So obviously it is a very critical need to reduce that reliance.

In terms of alternatives to diesel fuel, we do not have a lot of biomass in the State of Alaska. In parts of Alaska, of course, is that you have got these beautiful forested sections that must yield a lot of biomass, but that is not true in Village Alaska. If there is any wood in the region at all, it is typically just driftwood that is floating down the rivers from more biomass intense communities. So that does not become a very major alternative.

What we have seen happen is very high efficiency heating systems going on where typically you may get something in the order of 92 to 95 percent efficiency from a Toyostove, laser electric stove. Extensive efforts at weatherization of homes and businesses. We have actually partnered, we were able to get a very modest $200,000 from USDA for Rural Business Enterprise grants, and we have actually put together a commercial energy audit program because we believe that there are efficiencies of 30-plus percent to be gained in terms of the BTU content of space heating. That has moved ahead, and we have got some really good results from that that tell you what can be done to conserve heat. We believe that heat consumption can be reduced by a third or better just through energy efficiency and conservation measures.

We also utilize waste heat, so we recover heat from our diesel gensets. It is a very high priority for us to recover that heat and to distribute it to typically public buildings that are nearby the power plant. We are looking right now at what we can do to recover wasted heat from exhaust systems. That is 30 percent of the heat utilization of a genset. It comes out of the exhaust system or is just wasted up there. So we are looking to recover that as well, the objective being to drive down the overall consumption of diesel in a specific community.

There are some biomass combined heat and power projects that are very much experimental, emerging technology. We do have some of those installed across rural Alaska, and we are hopeful that they are going to yield some good results.

We are also looking at heat pumps. That typically, though, is really more viable in the more temperate parts of Alaska, so in south central. I am sure you are aware of the seawater heat pump system that they have in Seward. That is a technology that is potentially transferable. I believe that heat pump technology is progressing rapidly. I think we are going to see more air-to-air heat conversion where you can utilize recycled heat within a building.

But those are all the emerging technologies, and those emerging technologies have to be carefully fostered for them to develop into something that is commercially viable across a broad scale. Once they are commercially viable, the cost becomes much more affordable, and then they can be deployed much more ubiquitously.

The CHAIRMAN. Yes. I was out in Kwigillingok and was able to celebrate with the community there. I think it was either their first or their second day of being completely diesel free. They had three wind turbines, and the wind was kicking up. They had a little battery storage unit that was not much to speak of in terms of size, and then they had—I believe there were 25 different clay heating stoves within the homes, and you go inside roasty toasty.

But you think about just this little microcosm out there in an area where your costs up to this point are almost prohibitive for sustainability of a village, and you see what they are doing. I was in Egegik last week where they are putting in a run of river hydrokinetic turbine. It is going to be in the river. It should be in right now. It was in last year for a brief moment in time.

Again, a private entity is making this investment and realized that they needed to reconfigure. They went out and adjusted it. It is going to be back in the water and plugged into Egegik by the 15th, so that is just in a few days. You combine that with the five wind turbines that they have, the solar panels that they have, and, again, a sustainable community where they have struggled for so many years.

Mr. Hodge, you mentioned Kodiak. Kodiak is an amazing example of how you can utilize all of your renewable assets, whether it is the wind, the hydro. They are blessed with great hydro out there, but this is a major seaport, a major fishing community. To know that they, too, can be off diesel is a future for them that is really quite vibrant.

I think about all the technologies that we have being considered in laboratories, and how you work to get them to commercialization. And I say, okay, that is nice. We are actually making things happen on the ground. I think that some of our laboratories should be looking to what we are pioneering because we have to, because the alternatives are just not working for us. You cannot be a sustainable community if folks cannot afford the heat or the electricity, so you figure it out.

Sometimes it takes a little bit of duct tape. Sometimes it takes begging for dollars from the state, and the tribes, and the feds. But you piece it together with some really, really bright innovative people and through your universities. We are blessed with the University of Alaska, and I am sure we are where you are, Dr. Underwood, in Guam. But we are really pioneering this whole concept of microgrid, and Senator Cantwell and I were just talking back here about we have got this very generous eye to the rest of the world in how we can help facilitate energy solutions in Africa and elsewhere.

Again, I think to a certain extent charity begins at home, and I recognize that we definitely have energy needs that are not being met yet, but with a little bit of assistance, and I think looking to the experts, looking to the innovators, this is where it is really happening. And so, I commend you all.

Mr. Glick, you have got a high standard up there to reach Hawaii's renewable energy goals, how you are going to be dealing with the distributed generation aspect of it and the integration of all of your renewables. Many in the country are looking to you for the example and the leadership. You are kind of pioneering here, so we wish you well in that and are eager to know how we can be helpful and be off assistance.

Meera, you mentioned resourcing and some of the programs that are out there, and we have had a little bit of conversation about that today. We have a Renewable Energy Deployment Fund, a fund that I established through legislation some years ago. It is a nice idea, but you have got to have the dollars that are in it so that we can help our states, we can help our territories, so we can help make a difference and making sure that there is a level of sustainability that our economies can thrive.

I appreciate the leadership from each of you and the opportunity for you to share a little bit of the best practices and some of the challenges. Hopefully you inspire not only others, but you have learned from one another and you are going to take some good ideas back to Guam, the Caribbean, Alaska, Hawaii, and throughout all of our areas here.

With that, I thank you all, and we stand adjourned.

[Whereupon, at 11:44 a.m., the hearing was adjourned.]

APPENDIX MATERIAL SUBMITTED

U.S. Senate Committee on Energy and Natural Resources
July 14, 2015 Hearing: Islanded Energy Systems
Questions for the Record Submitted to the Honorable Esther Kia'aina

Questions from Ranking Member Maria Cantwell

Question 1: Overcoming Financing Barriers

During your testimony you indicated that the territories face challenges when seeking the resources required to execute their strategic energy plans.

You stated The Office of Insular Affairs (OIA) is responsible for coordinating Federal policy relating to the territories of Guam, American Samoa, the United States Virgin Islands (USVI), and the Commonwealth of the Northern Mariana Islands (CNMI), and accordingly you are in a good place to have a broad view of the challenges of the territories.

Question 2: Have you found instances where federal programs exist, such as the DOE loan programs, which could provide resources to support the islands' strategic energy plans if the programs were slightly modified to make territorial projects eligible?

Answer: The Office of Insular Affairs (OIA) has found that limited funding is available from other federal programs to support the islands' strategic energy plans.

The U.S. Department of Energy (DOE) Loan Programs Office administers two programs: the Title XVII Innovative Clean Energy loan program and the Advanced Technology Vehicles Manufacturing direct loan program. These are competitive loan programs that require at least $150,000 up front in loan application fees. Given the small size of the territorial energy projects, the loan application fees are cost prohibitive for the territories. The DOE loan programs are designed for much larger projects that accelerate the development of clean energy across the United States. DOE's smallest loan under the program is currently $50 million. While the DOE loan programs play an important role in supporting the deployment of renewable energy in states, major modifications would need to be made to the program to make it accessible to the U.S. territories.

The U.S. Department of Agriculture's Rural Utilities Service (RUS) loan program, on the other hand, is a viable financing mechanism for energy projects in the territories. However, loans sometimes do not cover the full cost of a project and territorial governments often face challenges of credit history and an inability to secure local matching funds. The loan programs sometimes require a labor-intensive application process and the loan funds can sometimes only be used for certain cost items. In addition, the territories at times must compete against much larger entities in the states for funding. For these reasons, grant programs are typically preferred over loan programs in the insular areas.

Due to the lack of funding sources for the U.S. territories, OIA proposes the creation of a new grant program within DOE designed to serve the unique needs of the insular areas in the implementation of their strategic energy plans. DOE possesses the expertise, technical capacity, and other resources to administer a program of this nature.

If such a program cannot be created, then OIA proposes a substantial increase to its existing Empowering Insular Communities (EIC) grant program of $3 million. The President's Budget for fiscal year 2016 proposes an increase to $4.4 million in EIC funding. This increase will not only allow OIA to continue the implementation of strategic energy plans in the four territories but will also assist with the development of a strategic energy plan in Puerto Rico. Should an energy plan for Puerto Rico be completed, significant funding would be needed in future years for the implementation of such a plan.

In summary, as Puerto Rico's population is nearly ten times that of the other four U.S. territories combined, there is concern that the inclusion of Puerto Rico in OIA's EIC grant program will have significant adverse impact our ability to help the other territories without an increase in our base funding of $3 million.

U.S. Senate Committee on Energy and Natural Resources
July 14, 2015 Hearing: Islanded Energy Systems
Questions for the Record Submitted to the Honorable Robert Underwood

Questions from Ranking Member Maria Cantwell

Question 1: Workforce and Financing Barriers

Two barriers to improving reliability and affordability of energy services in remote communities are a lack of technical expertise to operate and maintain alternative technologies and a lack of funding/financing to upgrade or replace existing equipment.

> **Question 1.1:** Would you please comment on how you view these two challenges and what partnership role you believe the federal government could play in helping you overcome them?

> **Question 1.2:** Are there other significant barriers that we should be aware of?

Question 2: Efficiency Improvements

The cheapest and most available energy resource is energy efficiency.

Would you please describe the efforts that have been taken in Guam to cut waste and improve the efficiency of the existing energy systems?

Question 3: Tools to Fund Efficiency Improvements

Energy Savings Performance Contracts (ESPCs) are financing tools widely used to fund energy efficiency projects. Under ESPCs, private energy service companies design, install, and finance energy system improvements in exchange for a portion of the guaranteed cost savings. However, because of high upfront costs, these companies prefer large government contracts.

> **Question 3.1:** Could you describe any experience you have had with ESPCs?

> **Question 3.2:** Has there been a role for government in Guam promoting the use of ESPCs?

> **Question 3.3:** Beyond ESPCs what steps do you see as being crucial to meeting your strategic energy plan goals and what do you see as the federal role in meeting those goals?

U.S. Senate Committee on Energy and Natural Resources
July 14, 2015 Hearing: Islanded Energy Systems
Questions for the Record Submitted to Mr. Mark Glick

Questions from Ranking Member Maria Cantwell

Question 1: Workforce and Financing Barriers

Two barriers to improving reliability and affordability of energy services in remote communities are a lack of technical expertise to operate and maintain alternative technologies and a lack of funding/financing to upgrade or replace existing equipment.

Question 1.1: Would you please comment on how you view these two challenges and what partnership role you believe the federal government could play in helping you overcome them?

Hawaii State Energy Office (HSEO) Response:
Technical Expertise to Operate and Maintain Alternative Technologies
Technical expertise is a critical issue to address but can also be an opportunity for Hawaii. Hawaii has recognized the need to develop a workforce pool with the expertise to support indigenous clean energy policy objectives. This need is being addressed as a Commitment to Action under the Clinton Global Initiative that engages local stakeholders including the State of Hawaii, University of Hawaii Manoa, Honolulu Community College, Hawaiian Electric, Hawaii Natural Energy Institute and the Blue Planet Foundation on a comprehensive clean energy workforce training and outreach effort. The Hawaii Statewide Modern Grid-Workforce Training Deployment commitment aims to prepare a next-generation workforce in technical skills needed to assist Hawaii's in its goals to deploy a statewide network of advanced metering infrastructure (AMI) by 2020 and to achieve 100% renewable energy by 2045.

The purpose is to recruit and retain students in a wide variety of training exercises that will enable them to build and operate the modern electrical grid as contractors and/or consultants to the utilities or to firms supporting utility AMI installations, development of renewable energy resources, demand response, storage options, and electric drive transportation and associated technologies.

Federal support of workforce educational programs can support the successful development of a local talent pool. Federal support could come in a variety of ways through things such as scholarships, resources and opportunities for students through National Renewable Energy Lab (NREL). Using Hawaii as a test bed for clean technology pilots with federal support would assist Hawaii in building a skilled clean technology workforce.

Lack of Funding/Financing to Upgrade or Replace Existing Equipment
The federal government has a meaningful role in supporting direct funding or loans to significant energy system upgrade projects that can help move the needle in the transition of Hawaii's energy system. While the benefits of renewable energy and energy efficiency to achieve energy self sufficiency and resiliency are clear, upfront infrastructure costs may be a barrier to a timely and cost effective transition.

U.S. Senate Committee on Energy and Natural Resources
July 14, 2015 Hearing: Islanded Energy Systems
Questions for the Record Submitted to Mr. Mark Glick

Question 1.2: Are there other significant barriers that we should be aware of?

HSEO Response: One of the most significant barriers is changing the mindset in how energy system planning is approached. Two-thirds of Hawaii's fossil fuel imports are for the transportation sector. Decarbonizing this sector will naturally put more pressure on the electric sector making coordination and implementation all the more important.

Analyzing the benefits and costs requires understanding the interdependencies in the energy eco-system. To effectively implement policy requires commitment from key stakeholders in all sectors to take a broader perspective when approaching cost benefit analysis of projects in their individual energy sectors so that opportunities are not missed, such as the benefits of electric drive charging and hydrogen production in reducing storage requirements. Alternatively, a lack of coordination could create additional electric system stress, for example if customers charge their cars as soon as they arrive home exacerbating the "duck curve" as evening peak demand increases.

Careful consideration of a market structure and accurate price signals that encourage customers to efficiently manage their energy use can help lower customers' bills while creating lower overall system costs. Accurate prices based on actual costs of doing business help spur innovation as companies look at ways to provide value propositions to customers that simultaneously solve energy system needs by balancing demands and lowering energy consumption. Innovation from accurate prices can occur for traditional electric loads through smart appliances that provide demand response or for new demands such as electric drive vehicles.

Federal support for infrastructure that supports or can take advantage of accurate price signals such as electric drive charging systems for electric and hydrogen vehicles can benefit both long term electric system load balancing and the decarbonization of the transportation sector. Federal support for such infrastructure will also provide confidence to the market place to invest in clean energy solution in Hawaii.

Question 2: Efficiency Improvements

The cheapest and most available energy resource is energy efficiency. Would you describe the efforts you have taken to cut waste and improve the efficiency of your existing energy systems?

HSEO Response: The HSEO has taken a multi-prong approach, including regulatory interventions, programs, and initiatives, to cut waste and improve the efficiency of our existing energy systems. Following are several relevant examples:

U.S. Senate Committee on Energy and Natural Resources
July 14, 2015 Hearing: Islanded Energy Systems
Questions for the Record Submitted to Mr. Mark Glick

- **Demand Response Regulatory Intervention**
  In response to the Hawaiian Electric Companies Integrated Demand Response Portfolio Plan (IDRPP)[1], the state Department of Business, Economic Development and Tourism (DBEDT) filed comments with the Hawaii Public Utilities Commission indicating that the IDRPP does not go far enough and is missing key details that make an evaluation difficult (i.e. HECO substitutes summaries and narratives for detailed analysis) and does not appreciate the sense of urgency required to meet and exceed the State's policy objectives. DBEDT suggested the following: (1) a detailed explanation to the Commission of how demand reduction or other benefits are measured with respect to each program, along with all assumptions and calculations; (2) a detailed explanation of why each program in the portfolio is a cost-effective means by which to achieve one or more of the portfolio goals; and (3) a detailed account comparing the costs and benefits of ancillary and other grid support services provided by each program as compared to using conventional fossil-fuel generation. The Commission has been reviewing the IDRPP and the comments from the docket interveners to determine whether or not it is in compliance with the Demand Response Policy Statement and consistent with other filings required by the Commission, notably the Power Supply Improvement Plans for each of the HECO Companies and the Distributed Generation Interconnection Plan (DGIP)[2].

- **Retirement of old power plants**
  Docket No. 2011-0206, Order No. 32053 mandated the Hawaiian Electric Company submit a Power Supply Improvement Plan which was to include a Fossil Generation Retirement Plan. In addition to this compulsory analysis, the Commission explained that, "at a minimum," HECO's Fossil Generation Retirement Plan was to: (1) analyze the potential roles that each fossil generating unit should play in the future; (2) analyze future fuel expenses, O&M expense, and capital expenditures that would be avoided if each existing fossil unit were retired; (3) consider the impact of each retirement, without replacement, on adequacy of power supply and reserve margins under existing capacity planning criteria; (4) analyze how the capacity value of solar, wind, energy storage, and DR resources will be factored into the determination of the adequacy of power supply; (5) analyze the feasibility of using existing sites to locate new, quick-start, fuel-efficient, flexible generation; and (6) discussion of the action plans, costs, and ratepayer impacts of implementing the Fossil Generation Retirement Plan.

  HSEO's analysis and discussion on HECO's Fossil Generation Retirement Plan was geared toward ensuring that the commission's requirements were met, that our clean energy policies were upheld, and that the utility provides a power plant retirement plan

---

[1] "Integrated Demand Response Portfolio Plan (IDRPP)", which HEI Companies (HE) filed in response to PUC's Order No. 32054 filed on April 28, 2014, Docket No. 2007-0341.
[2] Page 13, Order No. 32660, Docket No. 2007-0341.

U.S. Senate Committee on Energy and Natural Resources
July 14, 2015 Hearing: Islanded Energy Systems
Questions for the Record Submitted to Mr. Mark Glick

that would reasonably lead to significant energy efficiency savings and overall energy system improvements.

- **Public Benefits Fee Administrator Programs**
  Hawaii has established funding and programs using a Public Benefits Fee (PBF) or surcharge on utility sales that is administered by a PBF Administrator (PBFA). Current statute puts the PBFA under the auspices of the Public Utilities Commission. In FY 2015 the PBFA will have about $38 million in ratepayer funding to support energy efficiency programs. HSEO assisted the Commission and its oversight of the PBF/PBFA through activities such as securing a National Governors Association Retreat in 2014 to discuss bold and innovative PBFA programs in other states and the latest ideas regarding use of ratepayer funds to promote energy efficiency. HSEO staff also serve on the Commission's PBFA Technical Advisory Group as well as the Commission's Energy Efficiency Technical Working Group to promote energy efficiency.

  Hawaii's Energy Efficiency Portfolio Standard (EEPS) statute requires that by 2030 annual energy savings amount to 4,300 GWh reduction (approximately 30%) of annual electricity sales statewide. At the end of 2014, Hawaii had achieve a 17.3% reduction under the EEPS (vs. 15.7% in 2013) in advance of the 15% EEPS 2015 interim goal.

- **State Lead by Example Programs**
  Under the HSEO's Lead by Example program State of Hawaii public buildings and facilities are under consistent review and analyses to make sure they are as energy efficient as possible. A primary objective of Lead by Example is to protect the state against escalating energy costs and to expedite energy security to protect Hawaii and our economy against the volatility of world oil markets.

  Following are some highlights of our programs:
  o In 2014 for the third consecutive year, the State of Hawaii was awarded the Energy Services Coalition's *Race to the Top* in recognition for leading the nation in per capita performance contracting for state and county buildings. Over $315 million in performance contracts have been signed in both State and County with cost savings expected to grow to more than $830 million over the 20-year life of the contracts.
  o In December 2013, the State Department of Transportation entered into the largest single state performance contract in the nation: a $151 million energy savings contract which guaranteed reduction of energy use by 49 percent and $496.2 million guaranteed savings in energy costs; actual savings realized are estimated to be 8 percent higher.
  o State Office Tower Certifie LEED Gold. In 2012 the SOT was the first large office building, public or private, in the state to be certified Gold under LEED for Existing Buildings: Operations and Maintenance.

U.S. Senate Committee on Energy and Natural Resources
July 14, 2015 Hearing: Islanded Energy Systems
Questions for the Record Submitted to Mr. Mark Glick

- o A total of 29 state buildings are LEED certified or pending certification. An additional 43 LEED projects are in the process toward the goal of certification. There are currently over 30 LEED Accredited Professionals on staff at six state agencies; Department of Accounting and General Services; Department of Business, Economic Development, and Tourism; Department of Education; Department of Transportation; Hawaii Public Housing Authority; and the University of Hawaii.
- o Some 21 state buildings have received ENERGY STAR® awards, acknowledging that they rank in the top 25% of similar buildings nationwide.
- o DBEDT is implementing a U.S. Department of Energy Cooperative Agreement to benchmark and verify more than 552 eligible state department buildings with Energy Star Portfolio Manager.
- o A total of nearly 5.2 MW of photovoltaic generating capacity has been installed at various statewide airports. An additional 2.69 MW is pending.

- **Building Code Development and Updates**

DBEDT is a voting member of the statutorily established State Building Code Council (SBCC) which meets regularly to update various state codes such as the electrical, plumbing, fire, and energy codes. HSEO staff chairs the Energy Code Subcommittee. On July 7, 2014, the SBCC voted to adopt the latest updated International Energy Conservation Code (IECC) 2015, with Hawaii Amendments, as well as to adopt the Hawaii Residential Tropical Zone Code which was requested by the International Codes Council. The updated IECC 2015 and the Hawaii Residential Tropical Zone Codes must now be adopted by Administrative Rules and by the various county councils. HSEO will support and push for adoption of the Energy Code and also provide training and technical support to all state and county code officials and design professionals to ensure a smooth path to adoption and implementation of the new energy building code.

Question 3: Tools to Fund Efficiency Improvements

Energy Savings Performance Contracts (ESPCs) are financing tools widely used to fund energy efficiency projects. Under ESPCs, private energy service companies design, install, and finance energy system improvements in exchange for a portion of the guaranteed cost savings. However, because of high upfront costs, these companies prefer large government contracts.

Question 3.1: Could you describe any experience your communities have had with ESPCs?

HSEO Response: HSEO provides technical assistance to state and county agencies who select to implement performance contracting for energy efficiency and renewable energy implementation. To date over $315 million in performance contracts have been signed by state agencies; these agreements will bring over $830 million in energy savings over the life of the contracts. The State of Hawaii has for three straight years been awarded the Energy Services Coalition's *Race to the Top* award for the state with the highest per capita of performance

U.S. Senate Committee on Energy and Natural Resources
July 14, 2015 Hearing: Islanded Energy Systems
Questions for the Record Submitted to Mr. Mark Glick

contracting contracts. The Energy Services Coalition is a nonprofit organization composed of public and private entities committed to increase energy performance contracting. We are presently working with other agencies to increase the number of contracts and savings.

Question 3.2: Beyond ESPCs what steps do you see as being crucial to meeting your energy action plan goals and is there a federal role in meeting those goals?

HSEO Response: Continued funding and support of the State Energy Program (SEP) is essential for both supporting our building code updates and for supporting performance contracting. DBEDT notes that dedicated funding under the SEP Formula Grants is preferred to provide consistent support for recurring activities in such areas as building code improvements and ESPC technical assistance.

Question 4: USDA Funding for Rural Utilities

Question 4.1: With respect to funding and financing to upgrade your energy systems, would you please describe the role that the Rural Utilities Service (RUS) of the USDA plays in financing utilities projects in your communities?

HSEO Response: USDA RUS has been an important source of debt financing for the Kauai Island Utility Cooperative (KIUC) for its utility scale renewable energy projects. Among the larger projects funded by KIUC through the RUS was Kauai's largest solar energy project, a 10 MW PV and battery project storage project that received $68 million in RUS support. KIUC is the state's only cooperatively owned utility.

Question 4.2: Are RUS loans helpful, and are they flexible enough for your unusual circumstances and needs?

HSEO Response: KIUC uses USDA RUS as one of its primary financing options, but the electric utilities located on Maui, Hawaii Island, Molokai and Lanai do not have the same access, as subsidiaries of a much larger, for-profit company based in Honolulu. Perhaps consideration can be given to making financing options available to rural subsidiaries of larger, for-profit organizations with certain terms and conditions that would require benefits derived from such financing would have to be passed on to the community. The ultimate goal for USDA RUS should he to ensure that its low-cost financing has impact on the people that live in the rural community, regardless of who the intermediary is that deploys the financing and how big or small they are.

Question 5: Overcoming Financing Barriers

Mr. Glick, I note from your biography that you were instrumental in establishing the Hawaii Green Infrastructure Authority and the low-interest bond energy finance program.

As we have heard from the Witness from Alaska, states have increasingly been playing a more central role in ensuring that new energy technologies are deployed efficiently and quickly, but

U.S. Senate Committee on Energy and Natural Resources
July 14, 2015 Hearing: Islanded Energy Systems
Questions for the Record Submitted to Mr. Mark Glick

notes that the federal government has a role to play in assisting states in this area. For example, in Ms. Kohler's written testimony, she stated that:

"The State has established low cost financing options for energy infrastructure for larger utilities. The State funds research opportunities for emerging energy technologies.

> *But the State cannot carry all of the necessary infrastructure development with its limited resources. I plead with you as you consider a comprehensive energy bill that you include revisions to USDOE's loan program that is currently geared toward "innovative non-commercial" technologies. It should be looking instead at deploying innovative commercially viable technologies, such as what we are trying to do on a small scale."*

Question 5.1: Under your leadership, Hawaii has been a leader in establishing state financing mechanisms to provide access to capital for the deployment of efficient and clean energy technologies. As we look to encourage other states to follow your lead, do you think that the Department of Energy can be helpful in facilitating that deployment, per Ms. Kohler's suggestion? Is there a role here for the DOE Loan Programs Office?

HSEO Response:

The DOE Loan Program Office's current mission of deploying innovative and advanced clean energy technologies at scale, has provided access to companies that are innovating and deploying in the clean energy space. Consideration should also be given to providing financing access for intermediaries that deploy clean energy technology in communities and have the potential to make meaningful impact. Such programs also may have lower transaction costs and greater flexibility than the DOE Loan Program Office. For state and local programs that are attempting to ensure clean energy technologies are deployed and installed in communities, making capital available or connecting these sources to the capital markets that can provide low-cost capital is crucial.

Not all states and local programs are able to access private capital or allocate public funds toward clean energy deployment, helping states gain access to financing and setup loan programs to deploy funds would greatly impact the deployment of clean energy, especially in states where it may not be one of the top priorities.

Question 5.2: Are there other existing Federal energy loan or grant programs that could help you overcome financing barriers if they have greater flexibility to meet your unusual needs?

Please describe your current ability to finance implementation of projects identified in your state energy EEPS or RPS standards, and whether access to Federal financing would significantly help your efforts to increase the affordability and reliability of electricity?

U.S. Senate Committee on Energy and Natural Resources
July 14, 2015 Hearing: Islanded Energy Systems
Questions for the Record Submitted to Mr. Mark Glick

HSEO Response:

Currently, federal loan programs are not necessarily accessible to state entities wanting a larger pool of capital to seed clean energy technology deployment programs, and grants are also limited in amounts and must be used for very specific purposes with little flexibility for changing/expanding scope. In order for states to create meaningful financing programs for clean energy technology deployment, where it has sufficient scale to be impactful, there needs to be flexibility for program development and implementation, so that programs and offerings can be adjusted as changes occur.

The reason the Green Energy Market Securitization Program went to the private market for its initial capital infusion was because there were no requirements or limits imposed by bondholders on what the clean energy financing program must do and who it must serve in order to access the capital, all of that was open to the state to design and change so long as local stakeholders, such as the state Public Utilities Commission agreed, and there was a source to repay the bonds.

U.S. Senate Committee on Energy and Natural Resources
July 14, 2015 Hearing: Islanded Energy Systems
Questions for the Record Submitted to Mr. Hugo V. Hodge, Jr.

Questions from Ranking Member Maria Cantwell

Question 1: Workforce and Financing Barriers

Two barriers to improving reliability and affordability of energy services in remote communities are a lack of technical expertise to operate and maintain alternative technologies and a lack of funding/financing to upgrade or replace existing equipment.

> **Question 1.1:** Would you please comment on how you view these two challenges and what partnership role you believe the federal government could play in helping you overcome them?
>
> With regards to technical expertise, the Virgin Islands Water and Power Authority faces no obstacles as it pertains to obtaining qualified and competent individuals with technical experience. This is due to the close geographic location of the islands to the continental United States, and the fact that VIWAPA established a scholarship program, more than two decades ago, for high school students to pursue a degree in any of the engineering disciplines. The scholarship recipients, as a requirement of the agreement, must return to the Authority to work for the number of years that it took them to acquire the degree. As such the Authority has been able to attract and retain qualified employees in the technical fields.
>
> As it relates to funding to upgrade/replace existing equipment, this poses a challenge to VIWAPA. Currently the majority of funds for projects of these types come from the issuance of bonds. With declining sales and revenues, and the high costs associated with the cost of upgrading and replacing the generating equipment, the Authority has to prioritize spending of its limited dollars.
>
> To the extent that grants or loans are available from the federal government to assist we ask that it is considered, in the creation of these grants or loans, that they include the insular areas. Many grant, are limited to the Continental US thereby excluding the Territories. Further when grants do include the Territories and other insular areas, the amount that is set aside is small when compared against the critical financial need that the insular areas have for projects that will bring relief from high energy costs. We believe giving the insular areas more access to compete for grant funds or loans that are carved out for their specific use would be of tremendous benefit. Any assistance that can be provided in this matter would be appreciated.
>
> **Question 1.2:** Are there other significant barriers that we should be aware of?
>
> No.

Question 2: Efficiency Improvements

The cheapest and most available energy resource is energy efficiency.

Would you please describe the efforts you have taken to cut waste and improve the efficiency of your existing energy systems?

With regard to energy efficiency, the Authority has made several major changes in its operations to improve efficiency. For over thirty years, the Authority produced potable water utilizing the Israel Desalinization Engineering ("IDE") technology, which is a process dependent on burning fuel oil to produce steam to desalinate seawater. Approximately 7% of every gallon of fuel oil purchased by the Authority was used by the IDE process to meet thermal demand for water production purposes. In the past, this technology was viable given the low cost of fuel and the fact that oil prices then were not subject to the volatility and fluctuating prices we experience in today's oil market. When oil prices became volatile, the Authority issued an RFP for an option that would result in the lowest production cost for potable water, while simultaneously maintaining a high quality of water to our customers. The procurement resulted in a contract with Seven Seas Water Corp. to produce water via the Reverse Osmosis or "RO" process. The RO project was selected in order to change the Authority's process of producing potable water at its generating facilities on both islands from a thermal dependent process. The change from the IDE process to the RO production technology has resulted in an approximate 50% reduction in the cost to produce water. By changing from IDE to RO, to produce potable water, the Authority no longer has to operate generating units for steam to produce water, and the steam that was used for potable water production is now used to enhance combine cycle operations via heat recovery steam generators.

In addition to the above, the Authority has retrofitted certain of its equipment to produce power through combined cycle operation mode, thereby making the production of power more efficient.

Additionally, we contract with the Original Equipment Manufacturer ("OEM") for the maintenance of machines and equipment to ensure the expected output in the most efficient and reliable manner.

Last but certainly by no means least, the Authority has commissioned the preparation of the Integrated Resource Plan (IRP) to be completed within the next sixty days. The IRP is a comprehensive decision support tool and road map for meeting the Authority's objective of providing reliable and least-cost electric service to all of our customers, while addressing the substantial risks and uncertainties inherent in the electric utility business. The IRP is developed with considerable public involvement from our local utility commission (the Public Services Commission), local VI Government agencies, customer and industry advocacy groups, project developers, and other stakeholders. The key elements of the IRP include: a finding of resource need, focusing on the first 10 years of a 20-year planning period; the preferred portfolio of supply-side and demand-side resources to meet this need; and an action plan that identifies the steps we will take during the next two to four years to implement the plan. With this plan, the Authority will have a roadmap for providing power at the lowest, most reliable and efficient means in the upcoming years.

Question 3: Tools to Fund Efficiency Improvements

Energy Savings Performance Contracts (ESPCs) are financing tools widely used to fund energy efficiency projects. Under ESPCs, private energy service companies design, install, and finance energy system improvements in exchange for a portion of the guaranteed cost savings. However, because of high upfront costs, these companies prefer large government contracts.

> **Question 3.1:** Could you describe any experience your communities have had with ESPCs?

To facilitate the Efficiency Improvement on the demand side, the Authority has developed VIEnergize ("VIeS") as a business unit of the Authority, in support of the USVI 60x25 (60% by 2025) clean energy goal. The intent of the program is to help customers implement energy efficiency and renewable energy projects. These efforts will reduce the demand for electricity, particularly peak-demand, based on the use of demand-side technologies and programs. In order to connect USVI-appropriate services and technologies with WAPA customers, VIeS is facilitating these services in partnership with the VIEnergize Services Network (VISN) of energy product and service providers, financiers, and other energy professionals. VIeS has provided services for a number of small businesses and government agencies to audit their facilities to determine what efficiencies can be realized from recommended energy and water conservation measures. The Authority charges a reasonable fee for these services.

> **Question 3.2:** Beyond ESPCs what steps do you see as being crucial to meeting your strategic energy plan goals and is there a federal role in meeting those goals?

The success of energy efficiency programs on the demand side requires funding. While measures can be recommended to improve efficiency and reduce energy costs, many customers in the Virgin Islands cannot afford the financial investment for these energy conservation measure. The cost of energy efficient measures such as solar water heaters, new energy efficient appliances, ultra-low flush toilets, etc. are beyond the cost of the average person in the Territory, where the median income is approximately $20,000 per year. Thus far, banks have not been responsive in this matter. The federal government can be of great assistance in this matter. One of the more successful program in this regard was developed under the American Recovery and Reinvestment Act of 2009. With funds from that program, the Authority participated with other Government

Agencies to offer customers a loan to purchase a solar water heater. VIWAPA facilitated the collection of money paid by the customer to repay the loan. Similar programs from the federal government aimed at assisting customer with purchasing appliances and other energy saving devices are recommended.

Question 4: USDA Funding for Rural Utilities

Question 4.1: With respect to funding and financing to upgrade your energy systems, would you please describe the role that the Rural Utility Service (RUS) of the USDA plays in financing utilities projects in your communities?

Pursuant to the Rural Electrification Act of 1936, the Electric Programs make direct loans and loan guarantees to electric utilities to finance the construction of: electric distribution, transmission, and generation facilities, including system improvements and replacements required to furnish and improve electric service in rural areas as well as demand side management, energy conservation programs, and on-grid and off-grid renewable energy systems. The Electric Programs also provide financial assistance to rural communities with extremely high energy costs to acquire, construct, extend, upgrade, and otherwise improve energy generation, transmission, or distribution facilities.

In January 2013, the Authority's 2013 Core Electric, Distribution Automation, AMI, and Communications Infrastructure work plan was found to be eligible projects for loan contract purposes. In February 2013, the Authority's Governing Board authorized the Authority to borrow $15,000,000 for a guaranteed Rural Utilities Services (RUS) Federal Financing Bank (FFB) Loan for the basis of the current construction Work Plan.

In June 2013, the Authority submitted its loan application in the amount of $15,000,000. In September 2013, the Authority received a status update on the loan stating that it was approved by the Assistant Administrator Loan Committee (AALC) but still needed to be approved by the Senior Loan Committee (SLC). During the most recent rate case (Docket 612), the Authority was granted $460,762 for Fiscal Year 2014 and $921,524 for Fiscal Year 2015 for debt service associated with the RUS loan.

Since the conclusion of the rate case, a new Administrator for the program was appointed which seemed to cause RUS to revisit many issues that were previously agreed upon. The Authority has been involved in a number of calls to review the loan once again. Most of the focus has been centered around how this loan would work in tandem with the Authority's existing bonds and the legal documents that govern them (Bond Resolution, Indenture, etc.) in regard to certain covenants, remedies and other features unique to the loan agreement for RUS. Much of the delay has been on the RUS side as they have taken a substantial amount of time to review changes or modifications during our negotiations.

On May 7th the Authority, in consultation with its Financial Advisor and Bond Counsel, submitted a summary presentation that compared the covenants under the RUS loan program against the covenants under the Senior Bond resolution as well as the additional security provided to RUS through other provisions included in the Senior Bond resolution (debt service reserve fund, trustee etc.). On June 25th, in a follow-up call, RUS team did not agree to remove the covenants unique only to RUS but instead lower the required targets for certain covenants. The times earned interest ratio (TIER) which originally had a target of 1.25x was lowered to 0.10x and the debt service coverage ratio (DSCR) which originally had a target of 1.25x was lowered to 0.75x.

The Authority has agreed to these revised targets, however, we are awaiting final legal review from RUS regarding remedies of default under loan versus the existing bonds outstanding.

Question 4.2: Are RUS loans helpful, and are they flexible enough for your unusual circumstances and needs?

RUS loans will be helpful if received, however we do not believe the process to be flexible enough when it comes to providing financing for municipal utilities, like VIWAPA. VIWAPA has pledged all electric revenues generated from the Electric System ("Electric Revenues") on a first lien basis, pursuant to its Electric Revenue Bond Resolution (the "Senior Bond Resolution"). VIWAPA has also pledged Electric Revenues on a subordinate lien basis pursuant to its Electric Revenue Subordinated Bond Resolution (the "Subordinated Bond Resolution").

Since RUS is required to lend only on a first lien basis, the loan must be issued, and secured, under the Senior Bond Resolution on a parity basis with the Authority's existing Senior Lien Bonds.

The Authority currently issues Senior Lien and Subordinate Lien Bonds, as well as bank facilities that may include term loans and lines or letters of credit secured by the Authority's General Fund. As a municipal utility, the Authority generates little to no operating surplus. The Authority's rates, fees and charges must be approved by the Virgin Islands Public Services Commission ("PSC").

The rate covenants proposed under the RUS program are geared more towards cooperatives and are untenable for the Authority rate structure. The Authority is working to convince RUS that there are certain central security features of the Authority's Senior Bond Resolution that have historically proven satisfactory to the public finance investment community and the rating agencies that rate the Authority's Bonds. We hope that RUS will determine that it has the protection it requires in issuing the Authority this loan.

U.S. Senate Committee on Energy and Natural Resources
July 14, 2015 Hearing: Islanded Energy Systems
Questions for the Record Submitted to Ms. Meera Kohler

Questions from Ranking Member Maria Cantwell

Question 1: Workforce and Financing Barriers

Two barriers to improving reliability and affordability of energy services in remote communities are a lack of technical expertise to operate and maintain alternative technologies and a lack of funding/financing to upgrade or replace existing equipment.

> **Question 1.1:** Would you please comment on how you view these two challenges and what partnership role you believe the federal government could play in helping you overcome them?

> **Answer 1.1:** Integrating alternative technologies in small communities is a very complex problem requiring highly skilled technical personnel. The smaller the local system, the more expensive it is to respond to operational and maintenance needs. As a result, down times are significantly longer, costs are significantly higher and the return on investment is much lower. It is difficult to demonstrate a positive benefit-to-cost ratio when installation and operation costs greatly exceed Lower-48 levels and uptime is considerably lower. Grant-funding hybrid generation systems and transmission connections and providing assistance in training technicians would be of great help.

> **Question 1.2:** Are there other significant barriers that we should be aware of?

> **Answer 1.2:** The dearth of transportation options play a critical role in driving up the cost of energy and all good and services. Shipping materials to the villages costs $2.00 per pound – a cost unheard of in any other US state or territory. Anything the federal government can do to make a material difference would be of tremendous value.

Question 2: Efficiency Improvements

The cheapest and most available energy resource is energy efficiency.

Would you please describe the efforts you have taken to cut waste and improve the efficiency of your existing energy systems?

Answer 2: AVEC has been a leader in adapting truck engines for prime power generation. We have consistently driven up efficiencies through design and testing processes. We have optimized our distribution systems to yield line losses amongst the lowest in the country at under 4%. We capture and use waste heat from the engines as practical to offset public facility heating fuel use. Our residential consumers use less than half as much electricity as other Alaskans and a third of that used in other states. The high

U.S. Senate Committee on Energy and Natural Resources
July 14, 2015 Hearing: Islanded Energy Systems
Questions for the Record Submitted to Ms. Meera Kohler

cost of electricity is a major driver of conservation, which is enhanced by our proactive customer education and support program.

Question 3: Tools to Fund Efficiency Improvements

Energy Savings Performance Contracts (ESPCs) are financing tools widely used to fund energy efficiency projects. Under ESPCs, private energy service companies design, install, and finance energy system improvements in exchange for a portion of the guaranteed cost savings. However, because of high upfront costs, these companies prefer large government or commercial contracts.

> **Question 3.1:** Could you describe any experience your communities have had with ESPCs?

> **Answer 3.1:** I know of no ESPCs or ESCOs that have expressed any interest in rural Alaska. AVEC has initiated energy audits for commercial customers that are paid for by the USDA Rural Business Enterprise Grant program but we do not yet have information on implementation by recipients. Since most efficiencies are to be gained from building heating and ventilation, retrofit costs are much higher and there isn't a "utility bill" per se as heating fuel suppliers are not utilities.

> **Question 3.2:** Beyond ESPCs what steps do you see as being crucial to meeting your energy conservation and renewable goals and is there a federal role in meeting those goals?

> **Answer 3.2:** Federal subsidies and incentives for energy audits of commercial and public buildings in particular would make a great difference in energy conservation targets. Assistance in driving down the installation and operating costs of renewables and hybrid generation systems would make them feasible in these micro-grid systems.

Question 4: USDA Funding for Rural Utilities

> **Question 4.1:** With respect to funding and financing to upgrade your energy systems, would you please describe the role that the Rural Utility Service (RUS) of the USDA plays in financing utilities projects in your communities?

> **Answer 4.1:** AVEC is a borrower of long-term RUS funds for utility plant although we have not borrowed from them in recent years as their rates are not competitive with private funders such as National Rural Utilities Cooperative Finance Corporation and CoBank. RUS is severely underfunded and unable to provide nimble and creative financing options for electric cooperatives. We have utilized their High Energy Cost Grant Program extensively and have found them to be very responsive. We have also used their RBEG program.

U.S. Senate Committee on Energy and Natural Resources
July 14, 2015 Hearing: Islanded Energy Systems
Questions for the Record Submitted to Ms. Meera Kohler

Question 4.2: Are RUS loans helpful, and are they flexible enough for your unusual circumstances and needs?

Answer 4.2: See response to 4.1 above. We strongly support additional funding for RUS to enable them to maintain the necessary staffing levels and programs to support rural communities like those in Alaska.

 American
Public Power
Association

Statement of the

AMERICAN PUBLIC POWER ASSOCIATION

Submitted to the

SENATE ENERGY AND NATURAL RESOURCES COMMITTEE

For the July 14, 2015

"Hearing on Energy and Infrastructure Challenges and Opportunities in Alaska, Hawaii and the U.S. Territories."

(Submitted July 28, 2015)

The American Public Power Association (APPA) appreciates the opportunity to provide the following statement for the record to the Senate Energy and Natural Resources Hearing for the July 14, 2015, hearing on "Energy and Infrastructure Challenges and Opportunities in Alaska, Hawaii and the U.S. Territories." APPA is the national service organization for the more than 2,000 not-for-profit, community-owned electric utilities in the U.S. Collectively, these utilities serve more than 48 million Americans in 49 states (all but Hawaii), the U.S. Virgin Islands, Puerto Rico, Guam, Northern Mariana Islands, and American Samoa. APPA was created in 1940 as a nonprofit, non-partisan organization to advance the public policy interests of its members and their customers. Our members provide reliable electric service at a reasonable price with appropriate environmental stewardship. Most public power utilities are owned by municipalities, with others owned by counties, public utility districts, states, and territories. APPA members also include joint action agencies (state and regional entities formed by public power utilities to provide them with wholesale power supply and other services) and state, regional, and local associations that have purposes similar to APPA. Collectively, public power utilities deliver electricity to one of every seven electricity consumers. We serve some of the nation's largest cities, including Los Angeles, CA; San Antonio, TX; Austin, TX; Jacksonville, FL; and Memphis, TN. However, most public power utilities serve small communities of 10,000 people or less.

APPA commends Chairman Murkowski for holding a forum that explores the challenges and opportunities for energy systems in Alaska, Hawaii, and the U.S. territories of American Samoa, Guam, the Northern Mariana Islands, Puerto Rico and the U.S. Virgin Islands. APPA supports the testimony submitted by Hugo V. Hodge Jr, the Executive Director of the Virgin Islands Water and Power Authority (VIWAPA). Mr. Hodge is a member of the APPA Board of Directors, and we look forward to working with him, the Senate Energy and Natural Resources Committee, and other stakeholders on important issues related to islanded energy systems.

Utilities that provide remote communities with electricity generate it primarily from expensive, imported diesel fuel. These utilities are very interested in diversifying their fuel sources and not relying so heavily on expensive diesel. To confront this challenge, utilities that serve islanded populaces are interested in exploring renewable energy sources that would not require the importation of fuel.

As Chairman Murkowski is well aware, Alaska is a leader in the development and operation of micro-grids. The state has between 200 to 250 permanently islanded micro-grids. These micro-grids range in size from 30kW to more than 100 MW (for larger, remote hydropower systems). Some of these micro-grids have existed for over 50 years and provide electricity to isolated, rural communities. Alaska's isolated hybrid micro-grids use renewable energy sources, such as wind, solar, hydro, biomass, and tidal currents, paired with diesel generation.

APPA is supportive of efforts to examine technologies that could potentially reduce dependence on diesel fuel, improve reliability, and lower the cost of electricity. S. 1227, introduced by Chairman Murkowski, would direct the Department of Energy (DOE) to develop an implementation strategy to promote the development of hybrid, micro-grid system technologies for isolated communities. It would also seek to leverage local capacity and knowledge in developing such systems. APPA believes DOE should work with isolated communities to promote the innovative use of hybrid micro-grids and supports Chairman Murkowski's bill directing it to do so. We respectfully urge the committee to include S. 1227 in the broader energy legislation it is developing.

Written Testimony of
T. Stephen Wittrig, PhD
Senior Advisor, Advanced Energy Systems
Clean Air Task Force
Before the
Committee on Energy and Natural Resources
United States Senate
July 14, 2015

My name is Steve Wittrig, Senior Advisor, Advanced Energy Systems for the Clean Air Task Force. The Clean Air Task Force is a non-profit environmental organization dedicated to catalyzing the development and deployment of low emission energy technologies through research and analysis, public advocacy leadership, and partnership with the private sector.

Before joining the Clean Air Task Force, I served at BP as Director, Advanced Technologies. During my 30-year career in the petroleum industry, I worked in research and development, marketing, strategy and projects in E&P, refining and chemicals. I was also a leader in strategy development and implementation for BP's Alternative Energy business. I hold a PhD in Chemical Engineering from Cal Tech.

This is an important and timely hearing for a variety of reasons. Given the emphasis on the realization of an intelligent, integrated power grid, "islanded" energy systems are often overlooked. Interestingly, "islanded" energy systems—whether we are referring to a remote village in Alaska or physical islands such as Hawaii, Guam or the Virgin Islands—offer opportunities to consider novel approaches to meeting everyday energy needs, not only with respect to electricity, but also with respect to heating, cooling, and transportation.

I would like to suggest that a ubiquitous, familiar chemical in global commerce—ammonia—could one day play an important role in such "islanded" energy systems, as well as situations where there is "stranded" natural gas and/or renewable energy—the precise situation faced by Alaska, Hawaii and many other places around the world. Further, existing fossil power generation stock (coal and oil power plants, combustion turbines, natural gas combined cycle power plants and large diesel gensets) could be shifted over time to be fueled by ammonia produced from low carbon sources. This would add an important technology option to the challenging task of decarbonizing the global energy system. For instance:

- Ammonia can be manufactured using natural gas or low/zero-carbon electricity sources including nuclear, fossil with carbon capture, and renewables including geothermal, solar and wind. Ammonia can then be used to power an internal combustion engine, a turbine, a boiler, or even a rocket engine. (During World War II, Belgians used ammonia to power their buses because oil was in such short supply. During the 1960s, the U.S. Air Force used anhydrous ammonia and liquid oxygen to power the rocket engine for the X-15.)
- Consequently, ammonia can be an energy storage strategy to balance intermittent, variable renewable energy production. Ammonia can be manufactured when solar and wind energy are available in abundance, and used to power a generator when they are not. Such an approach has obvious potential application in the context of a remote Alaska village or an island community, particularly if that community is reliant upon expensive and sometimes unreliable sources of imported fuel.

- Low-carbon ammonia could also be produced at large scale using nuclear power and fossil generation with carbon capture and geologic storage. Another potential path would be to produce ammonia at large gas fields and then capture and geologically store all ammonia production process CO_2.
- Ammonia can also serve as a superb hydrogen carrier. Ammonia has a high hydrogen content (17.65% of its mass) and can be converted directly to electricity in an alkaline fuel cell, or catalytically cracked to provide hydrogen for fuel cell vehicles.
- Ammonia is stored in relatively simple, inexpensive pressure vessels, similar to LPG. It is routinely distributed and used in agricultural communities across the US.
- Ammonia can be produced from natural gas at a cost of $10-$20 per MMBTU. Importantly, it can be economically delivered to a more diverse set of locations and stored at much lower cost than LNG or pipeline gas. This can offer the opportunity for clean, on-demand electricity to "islanded" economies around the world.
- And perhaps most interesting of all, no CO_2 is produced at the point of ammonia's use as a fuel. Other pollutants, such as the oxides of nitrogen that can be produced when ammonia is burned, are easily controllable. Moreover, if ammonia is manufactured using renewable energy, or if carbon capture is utilized when ammonia is produced using fossil fuel, ammonia offers a zero or near-zero carbon energy solution.

Ammonia can also be used to monetize stranded natural gas or renewable energy assets. On Alaska's North Slope, for example, one could envision using some of Alaska's currently stranded natural gas to make ammonia, yielding easily captured CO_2 from ammonia production for enhanced oil recovery (EOR) in North Slope oil fields. Shell Oil Company patents from the 1960's suggest that ammonia could be intermixed with oil and transported to market through the Trans-Alaska Pipeline, thus extending its economic life as North Slope production continues to decline. The produced ammonia might then be piped to interior Alaska for use as a heating fuel or for power generation, or distributed to remote villages to power modified diesel generator sets. Eventually North Slope ammonia might be marketable to Asian power generation companies currently operating on LNG and might even command a price premium given the low carbon content if produced with ammonia process CO_2 used for EOR.

I am not suggesting all of these opportunities are readily achievable and easily scalable at this moment. But I am suggesting that the use of ammonia, given its properties as a potentially zero carbon fuel; as a means to monetize stranded natural gas or to balance renewable energy; and as a way to offer a low or zero carbon fuel for power generation and transport in an "islanded" energy system, represent opportunities worthy of careful examination.

As with all fuels, ammonia has health and safety hazards as a chemical that must be dealt with. But it is chemically stable, less flammable than gasoline or LPG, and is used widely today in Alaska, Hawaii and other "islanded" communities for refrigeration and agriculture. The health and safety hazards are well documented over decades of experience and they are manageable with standard engineering practice.

Department of Energy has, in the past, examined the use of ammonia as an energy carrier, as a potential alternative fuel, and for other purposes. But it has only tended to do so on an ad hoc manner. I would respectfully suggest that the Committee, in the context of any energy legislation it develops over the coming months, should direct the Department to more actively consider the opportunities ammonia might play in the situations I have outlined above, or in contexts others may suggest. The potential applications in Alaska, Hawaii and other "islanded" energy situations strike me as particularly compelling and worthy of a dedicated, sustained research and development effort at the Department of Energy and other relevant government agencies.

If ammonia is part of the energy discussion, we might envision the day when remote villages or distant islands, who today pay exorbitant prices for imported and potentially unreliable sources of fuel, might control their own energy destiny by synthesizing their own ammonia fuel using locally available energy resources, water and air—potentially through a process that is substantially free of CO_2 emissions.

Thank you for the opportunity to submit this testimony for the hearing record, and I would be pleased to work with members and their staff in further exploring these ideas.

##

www.ingramcontent.com/pod-product-compliance
Lightning Source LLC
Chambersburg PA
CBHW081842280526

45789CB00007B/2544